HEALTHY
cooking
for one
COOKBOOK

HEALTHY
cooking for one
COOKBOOK

75 Delicious Recipes Made Simple

LAUREN O'CONNOR, MS, RDN

Photography by **ELYSA WEITALA**

ROCKRIDGE
PRESS

First Rockridge Press trade paperback 2021

Rockridge Press and the Rockridge Press logo are trademarks or registered trademarks of Callisto Media Inc. and/or its affiliates in the United States and other countries and may not be used without written permission.

For general information on our other products and services, please contact our Customer Care Department within the United States at (866) 744-2665, or outside the United States at (510) 253-0500.

Paperback ISBN: 978-1-64876-689-3 | eBook ISBN: 978-1-64876-186-7

Manufactured in the United States of America

Interior and Cover Designer: Angie Chiu
Art Producer: Hannah Dickerson
Editors: Lauren Ladoceour and Van Van Cleave
Production Manager: Michael Kay
Production Editor: Melissa Edeburn

Photography © 2021 Elysa Weitala. Food styling by Victoria Woollard.
All decorative icons used under license from The Noun Project.
Author photo courtesy of Violeta Meyners.

10 9 8 7 6 5 4 3 2 1

To my mom
for always believing in me.

contents

Introduction

THERE WAS A TIME IN MY LIFE WHEN I WAS COOKING FOR ONE—
just after college, pre-career, and around the time my husband and I first
started dating.

I was in my mid-20s and conscious of my health. I spent hours at the
gym, but I definitely ate takeout more often than not. I always intended to
eat healthy, and at the time I felt I was making good choices. My standard
diet consisted of instant oatmeal or a banana with peanut butter for breakfast, 6-inch whole-grain subs packed with extra veggies for lunch, and frozen
"healthy" entrées for dinner. I often splurged on delicious but expensive
takeout salads, like Chinese chicken salad and Greek salad, to make sure I got
plenty of greens.

My well-intentioned efforts weren't financially sustainable. My wallet was
thin, my credit card statements were getting high, and I was making no head-
way in paying off my school loans. So, I started hitting up the Sunday farmers'
markets to inspire home cooking, save money, and impress my then boyfriend.
Equipped with several cookbooks, I began working my way through standard
dishes and learning to cook for myself and eventually one other. Because
most cookbook recipes serve four or more, I had to cut ingredient amounts
in half. The good news: I was finding my way to better health and ultimately
my career path in the health field. I had found my purpose, and there was no
looking back.

Fast-forward: I am now a registered dietitian (10-plus years), a mother
of twin tweens, and a spouse. I'm the head cook of our family and no longer
cooking for one. But my experience and skill set have enabled me to work with
dozens of single patients who have improved their well-being by learning some
simple cooking-for-one strategies.

Healthy eating need not be expensive and time-consuming. I've gathered all my best tools to help you achieve better health simply, affordably, and deliciously. It takes only a little grocery-store savvy and kitchen know-how to get started on the path to a healthier you. The overall goal is to make home cooking doable and fun.

I do welcome occasional takeout or dine-in choices, but I always have a plan to keep it portion-controlled so I can incorporate leftovers into my healthy meals. For instance, one of my favorite recipes in this book is my Skillet Meatloaf (page 91), which allows for enough leftovers to make my Spaghetti Bolognese (page 92) the next day.

Follow this book's guidelines for sustainable choices that won't break the bank or keep you in the kitchen all day. Don't worry: You won't be hunting around or shopping online to buy fancy specialty ingredients. Rather, you'll learn how to create tasty, budget-friendly meals using tips for keeping produce fresh, preserving leftovers, and making complete meals from them. I even provide a meal plan to help you get started. So let's get cooking!

CHAPTER ONE

The Joy of Cooking for Yourself

Remember the first time you bit into a ripe peach with its fuzzy peel and sweet juices? Fond childhood memories can be rekindled once you start cooking for yourself. This chapter will show you how to keep your cooking not only waste-free but also healthy and tasty.

Parties of One

Perhaps you are a young adult, divorced or widowed, or an empty-nester. Whatever your circumstance, you can learn to make cooking for one sustainable and pleasurable.

Consider the benefits of preparing your own meals. You control your portions, you balance the foods on your plate (proteins, veggies, whole grains, healthy fats), and you make healthy meals just the way *you* like them. Finally, you save money when you don't rely on eating out—or ordering in.

Restaurant meals can be hard on your wallet and your health. They tend to be rich in animal protein and starch and therefore high in sodium, saturated fat, and calories. According to a 2012 article in *Nutrition Reviews*, eating out frequently is associated with excess body weight.[1]

Home cooking can be healthy, and it need not be challenging, even if you dine solo most of the time. It just takes a little forethought. The recipes in this book limit waste and put leftovers to good use.

So, grab an apron and get ready to reconnect with your food. When you establish a pleasurable relationship with food, healthy eating becomes not just attainable but also sustainable.

Healthy Delicious

Healthy delicious is a connection you definitely can achieve. When you sit down to enjoy food you've cooked using fresh, healthy ingredients, you are experiencing a pleasure tied to one of nature's perfect offerings. Again, let's go back to the humble peach. Peaches contain antioxidant nutrients that serve your body well, and they pair surprisingly well in a salad with dark leafy greens, such as spinach. Just think of them as an alternative to that other juicy fruit we use commonly in salads—the tomato. With my Spinach and Peach Salad with Avocado (page 37), you get the benefits of fruit and veggies in one tasty, simple dish.

And speaking of fruits and veggies, there are so many colorful combinations you can create with these foods. These naturally pigmented plants (think plums, bell peppers, carrots, broccoli, tomatoes, just to name a few) add to the taste and nutrition, too. You'll reap a variety of nutrients and get the nourishment you need and the visual and taste appeal you desire. Eating more plants contributes to improved health and can be deliciously appealing as well.

---

[1] Ilana N. Bezerra, Cintia Curioni, and Rosely Sichieri, "Association between Eating Out of Home and Body Weight." *Nutrition Reviews* 70, no. 2 (February 2012): 65-79. DOI.org/10.1111/j.1753-4887.2011.00459.x.

I consider fruits and veggies the ultimate living palette, a fantastic color wheel. With a variety of fruits and vegetables, you can't go wrong. And you'll still have room to enjoy meat, poultry, fish, and dairy. It's all about balance, portion control, and how you cook your foods. The benefit of cooking for yourself is that you are in control of everything.

Here are some simple guidelines to prepare meals that are both healthy and delicious:

- [ ] **CHOOSE BAKED OVER FRIED.**

- [ ] **BE WATCHFUL OF THE SODIUM CONTENT**—and I'm not just talking about the salt shaker. Relying too much on animal proteins, convenience foods, and frozen entrées can bump up your sodium intake, too.

- [ ] **FILL HALF YOUR PLATE WITH VEGGIES.**

- [ ] **AIM FOR 3 TO 4 OUNCES OF PROTEIN FOR YOUR ENTRÉE.**

- [ ] **ENJOY ABOUT ½ CUP OF WHOLE GRAINS** (or corn or potatoes) as part of each meal.

- [ ] **INDULGE IN FIBER-RICH FOODS** like veggies, whole grains, and/or legumes.

- [ ] **USE A LITTLE HEALTHY FAT** (such as olive oil) in the preparation of your protein.

- [ ] **FOR SALADS, INCLUDE HEALTHY FATS** like a quarter of a medium avocado, 2 to 3 tablespoons of nuts or seeds, and a light vinaigrette (or, more simply, oil and vinegar).

In the end, your plate should be colorful, full of texture, tasty, and satisfying.

Helpful Pointers

Over the years, I've seen many patients who need a just a bit more guidance when it comes to starting a healthy eating plan. They're on board for the benefits, yet they're still a little hesitant because they are cooking for just one. So, I've developed some tips and tricks to help them pursue their journey to better health.

1. **PLAN YOUR MEALS.** Create a loose menu plan for the week ahead. Focus mainly on your dinners, because lunches can easily be built from leftovers and breakfasts can be no-brainers. Having some meals in mind will also help you stay on track for healthy eating and prevent impulsive eating.

2. **LEVERAGE YOUR LEFTOVERS.** Creating a reimagined meal can be fun! Repurposing leftover pork chops from last night's dinner for a healthier version of fried rice the next day is a perfect example. Perhaps you've got a pile of mashed potatoes leftover from your Salisbury steak takeout (I won't tell). Use those potatoes to make potato pancakes to serve with a quick veggie scramble the next day.

3. **PREPARE ONE-POT MEALS.** Making an entire meal in just one pan is a great way to simplify your cooking and keep your dishwashing to a minimum. You'll have plenty of examples to follow in my recipe chapters, like my one-skillet Lemon Pepper Tilapia with Bell Peppers and Potatoes (page 71).

4. **MAKE THE MOST OF YOUR PANTRY.** Keep your pantry stocked with low-sodium canned foods (such as tomatoes, tomato paste, and beans), dried pasta, brown rice, quinoa, oats, nuts and seeds, dried fruits, cooking oils, and a variety of common seasonings. These basic ingredients will allow you to create efficient, tasty meals and snacks.

Essential Healthy Shopping Guide

This guide is designed with you in mind—the solo cook. The idea is to simplify your shopping, stock your kitchen wisely, and set you up for overall success. Foods are broken down by category (produce, meat and seafood, dairy, grains, and so on). Each category contains your best bets for shopping. You'll also get tips for choosing healthier ingredients and buying only what you'll need (no excess, no spoilage). It's a good idea to keep an eye out for single-serve portions of foods, but you won't be limited to scouting these out. That's where my storage tips come into play. I encourage you to shop with these notes and recommendations in mind.

PANTRY STAPLES

Whenever possible, try to purchase products that are simple and minimally processed—that is, without a lot of added sugars, preservatives, and artificial colors or flavorings. Instead of reaching for sugary cereals and snack items, you'll rely on whole food ingredients like oats, peanut butter, raisins, nuts and seeds, beans, and all your favorite spices (cinnamon, garlic, Italian seasoning, onion power, lemon pepper).

When you stock your pantry with healthy, shelf-stable staples, you'll have plenty to rely on even when your refrigerator seems bare.

BAKING STAPLES

All-purpose whole-wheat flour is useful for baking as well as for whipping up a quick gravy or thickening a soup.

Oats are ideal for baking cookies and muffins because they add fiber. They can also be used to replace bread crumbs in recipes like baked "fried chicken" or homemade fish sticks. Packets of unflavored instant oatmeal will help you make quick, portion-controlled breakfasts.

Semisweet or dark (70 to 80 percent) chocolate chips have less sugar than sweet chocolate chips.

Pure vanilla extract and ground cinnamon are a great way to add sweetness to your foods, especially when you are minimizing sugar in your diet. If you add honey or maple syrup (or even refined white sugar) to batter for baked goods, keep the amount minimal.

I recommend you store sweeteners on your top shelf so you aren't tempted to use them on a regular basis.

GRAINS AND BEANS

Whole-grain breads and brown rice contain more fiber than their lighter, more polished counterparts, white bread and white rice. Other great choices include quinoa, barley, couscous, farro, and whole-grain pasta—look for options with at least 3 grams of fiber per serving. You can opt for instant or quick-cooking varieties. For example, Trader Joe's carries a 10-minute farro. You can find instant brown rice in microwaveable or boil-in bags to save you time. But many regular whole grains generally take no longer than 20 minutes to prepare once your water is boiling.

When it comes to canned beans and legumes, you have plenty of choices, including black beans, kidney beans, chickpeas, lentils, and cannellini beans. Be sure to seek out lower-sodium varieties and always rinse them before use. Another great option is dried lentils, which don't take nearly as long to cook as other dried beans. If you can find lentils canned, even better.

DAIRY AND EGGS

Use low-fat milk and unsweetened low-fat or nonfat plain Greek yogurt. Yogurt is a versatile protein-rich option—you can use it as a creamy layer for berry parfaits, a sour cream substitute, a smoothie base, or a flavored dip.

Go for low-fat cheese whenever possible to add flavor and richness to your dishes. Whether you sprinkle a tablespoon of grated Parmesan onto your pasta with marinara or add a slice of low-fat cheddar or provolone to your turkey burger, cheese can make many meals even more satisfying. Single-serving cheese slices make portion control simple.

Nonfat ricotta is another great dairy option. Mix a bit with fresh fruit for a delicious, protein-packed snack or dessert. Or try it in my Ricotta Mac-n-Cheese with Spinach and Marinara (page 52).

Eggs are a great source of protein because they are quick and easy to make. Boiled eggs can be eaten as is or used to make egg salad or deviled eggs.

FRUITS AND VEGETABLES

Purchase fresh fruit individually—1 or 2 bananas, 1 or 2 apples at a time—to lessen your load and prevent waste. If you've bought too many bananas or stone fruits, peel and slice leftovers and store them in an airtight container in the freezer for smoothies. Leftover apple should be wrapped and stored in the refrigerator so you can add it to your oatmeal the next day. If buying canned fruits, choose those packed in 100 percent juice (or light syrup) and drain before using.

Keep a variety of leafy greens and nonstarchy veggies in your refrigerator for quick meals. I recommend spinach, romaine lettuce, broccoli, bell peppers, carrots, celery, and mushrooms. Buy veggies like bell peppers individually when you can.

Frozen fruits and veggies are also great choices because they are sealed at their peak of ripeness, which locks in their flavor—as well as their nutrients. Frozen broccoli or green beans can round out almost any meal. Packages of stir-fry blend, fajita blend, or mixed peas and carrots come in handy when you want to add a variety of veggies to your dish without a lot of prepping. Be sure these mixes aren't pre-seasoned; seasoned mixes may contain fat or sugar.

POULTRY

Purchase skinless chicken breasts or thighs. Although chicken breasts are leaner, thighs have more flavor and tend to be more satisfying. Chicken breasts are perfect for salads and sandwiches; thighs are great in soups and stews. Most chicken parts come in packages of at least four pieces. To save time and storage space, look for pre-cooked chicken breast strips in the refrigerator or frozen sections of your grocery store. Otherwise, tightly seal and store unused portions in your freezer for up to nine months.

Other healthy poultry options include ground turkey, turkey or chicken sausages, and turkey bacon. When using ground turkey, choose 70 percent less fat. Breakfast links are a convenient and portion-controlled choice—look for 70 percent less fat, nitrate-free, 100 percent turkey links. Turkey bacon (preferably 60 percent less fat and sodium) is another option. All of these products will keep fresh in the refrigerator for a week; freeze any remaining portions. You can crumble one slice of crisp turkey bacon on top of a salad for a little extra protein and flavor.

SEAFOOD

Dietary guidelines recommend you eat seafood twice a week because it is a protein source with beneficial omega-3 fatty acids. Select low-mercury seafood, such as sardines, trout, and shrimp. Other good seafood options include salmon, tilapia, and cod. Visit your grocery store's fish counter to get just the size and amount you need.

It's best to eat any leftover seafood the next day to enjoy its optimal flavor and texture. Fish tacos are a delicious way to enjoy leftover fish or shrimp. Another option: Toss any remainder into your next day's salad for some protein and omega-3s.

Canned tuna is another great option for its long shelf life, convenience, and small, portion-friendly containers.

MEAT

According to USDA guidelines, you should limit consumption of beef and pork to increase your focus on plant-based proteins. Choose meats that are at least 85 percent lean or extra-lean (93 percent lean). Tip: If the meat looks marbled, it's quite fatty. Grass-fed meat is recommended because it contains more B vitamins, antioxidants, and omega-3s than non-grass-fed meat. Organic and grass-fed meats are also recommended, but these meats are relatively costly. As long as you stick with lean cuts, you'll limit your exposure to antibiotics, hormones, and pesticide residues, which get stored in animal fat.

If you buy meat from your grocer's butcher counter, you can get just the amount you need for a meal, or you can include extra to allow for leftovers for the next day. You can also purchase a two- or four-pack of burger patties. Tightly seal and freeze the remaining patties for later use.

Minimizing Food Waste

1. **SAVE YOUR LEFTOVER HALF ONION.** You'll want to prevent it from drying out so you can use it in another recipe. Wrap it in plastic wrap and seal it tightly or use a resealable plastic bag to ensure it stays airtight. Refrigerate in your produce drawer for up to a week.

2. **KEEP THAT HALF A BANANA.** When a recipe for one requires only half a banana, peel the other half, place it in a resealable plastic bag, and freeze it for up to 3 months. You can use it for a single-serving smoothie whenever you please.

3. **TURN FAST-RIPENING FRUIT INTO DESSERT.** When those pears or plums are getting close to passing their prime, make them into a compote. Simply chop them up, put them in a saucepan, add a little water, and stew until warmed. Serve them over nonfat ricotta or low-fat Greek plain yogurt for a quick dessert (or add the stewed fruit to your morning oatmeal).

4. **FREEZE DARK GREENS.** Rinse and dry dark leafy greens such as kale, spinach, and basil, put them in a resealable plastic bag, and freeze them to use in smoothies or pasta. Stack fresh basil leaves, roll them tightly, and chop them finely. Put all the basil in a small bowl and coat thoroughly with a drizzle of oil, then transfer the mixture to an ice cube tray. Cover the tray with plastic wrap and put it in the freezer. Once the cubes are frozen, pop them out and store them in a resealable plastic bag in your freezer. Add the cubes to soups, stews, or sauces as needed.

5. **SALVAGE CELERY.** If you haven't quite gotten through that head of celery, fear not. You can chop it and lightly sauté it just as you would an onion. Add it to your next skillet recipe for a fiber boost.

Saucepans and the Solo Chef

Healthy cooking is easiest when you have the right kitchen equipment. You don't need fancy gadgets and equipment to make the recipes in this book. Here's what you will need:

6-INCH AND 10-INCH CERAMIC SAUTÉ PAN OR NONSTICK SKILLET: This pan or skillet will be your go-to for most dinners. Ceramic is a safer nonstick option than Teflon, which contains toxins.

MUFFIN TIN: This tin will be handy for making individual-size treats or savory portion-controlled meals such as egg cups or mini meatloafs.

RIMMED BAKING SHEET: A baking sheet is handy for baking cookies or toasting pitas or tortillas.

9-INCH GLASS BAKING DISH: This dish is the right size for a number of dishes, from oven-fried chicken to roasted veggies.

MIXING BOWLS: These bowls save space because they stack inside one another, and they are handy for everything from mixing up batter to tossing salad ingredients.

2-CUP LIQUID MEASURING CUP: Use this cup not just to measure liquids but also to beat eggs, prep a small amount of batter that can be poured directly into a pan, or whisk up a salad dressing.

A SET OF MEASURING SPOONS: Rather than eyeball your measurements, use exact measurements to maximize flavor and control the amount of fat and sodium in your dishes.

SPATULAS: A nylon or plastic spatula is perfect for flipping your French toast or scrambling eggs in your nonstick pan. Use a flexible silicone spatula to scrape batter off the sides of a bowl to minimize waste.

BLENDER: A reliable blender lets you whip up healthy smoothies in no time. And its quick blending action can also help you mix batter and puree soup.

CAN OPENER: Small and handy, this tool is essential for any recipe that calls for canned beans or tomatoes.

Recipes and Menus for You

From easy no-cook combos to one-skillet wonders, you can have many delicious meals ready in 30 minutes or less. The recipes in this book are designed to whet your appetite without keeping you waiting. But they are also created with your health in mind. With my guidelines, you'll be using just what you need and will have plenty of ways to leverage your leftovers.

One of my favorite recipes is Braised Tilapia with Bell Peppers and Sweet Peas (page 68) because it's so rich and flavorful. This one-skillet meal packs plenty of veggies!

For a restaurant-worthy upgrade from Hamburger Helper meals, try my Veggie and Ground Turkey Skillet (page 62). It tastes hearty, but it's actually waistline friendly with a mélange of chopped mixed veggies in the mix. (Hint: Using mixed frozen veggies such as peas, carrots, corn, and green beans is a real time-saver.) For a lovely leftover meal, serve it up sloppy joe–style on a whole-wheat bun. And if you're looking for something you can make in a jiffy, try my Saucy Bean Burrito Bowl (page 29)—a dish you can create with a few staples in your cupboard.

To make your cooking efficient and waste-free, I've prepared a week-long menu to help you enjoy wholesome, no-fuss meals that make good use of your leftovers.

Sunday

BREAKFAST: Yogurt Berry French Toast (page 18)

LUNCH: Braised Tofu "BLT" (page 40)

DINNER: Turkey Chili (page 90)

DESSERT: Blueberry-Mango Soft-Serve (page 109)

Monday

BREAKFAST: Scrambled Egg in a Mug (page 21)

LUNCH: Healthy Cobb Salad (page 32) with leftover tofu

DINNER: Leftover chili served on whole-wheat bun with EZ Coleslaw (page 99)

Tuesday	BREAKFAST: Banana-Pecan Oatmeal (page 19)
	LUNCH: Hearty Grain Bowl with Seasoned Black Beans (page 48)
	DINNER: Herbed Chicken Breast (page 87)

Wednesday	BREAKFAST: Strawberry-Banana Smoothie (page 17)
	LUNCH: Chicken Salad Pita (page 28) made with leftover chicken breast
	DINNER: Roasted Herb Shrimp with Chickpeas and Tomatoes (page 73)

Thursday	BREAKFAST: Grilled Peach and Ricotta Toast (page 25)
	LUNCH: Chickpea-Avocado Wrap (page 39)
	DINNER: Teriyaki Pork with Roasted Carrots and Broccoli (page 88)

Friday	BREAKFAST: Yogurt Berry Parfait (page 22)
	LUNCH: Saucy Bean Burrito Bowl (page 29) made with leftover carrots and broccoli
	DINNER: Lemon Pepper Tilapia with Bell Peppers and Potatoes (page 71)

Saturday	BREAKFAST: Savory Eggs with Greens and Grains (page 16)
	LUNCH: Tuna Niçoise Salad (page 31)
	DINNER: Five-Spice Pork Chops with Chickpea "Fried Rice" (page 84) made with leftover pork

The Company You Keep

You might get quite used to cooking for one (and you should be proud). But having someone over for a meal need not be daunting. It can be as simple as adding more veggies and a little creativity.

One of my clients, a young college student who grew up in foster care, struggled with her weight. "Miss E" was a self-proclaimed convenience store junkie and a regular at her local pizza joint. With my guidance and support, she learned to cook healthfully (and practically) for herself. She lost more than 20 pounds over the course of 6 months.

Miss E was getting comfortable cooking for one, but the prospect of preparing a healthy meal for herself and her boyfriend seemed daunting. On Friday night dates, they ate two separate meals: he, pizza; she, a healthy standard like herbed chicken breast, steamed carrots, and brown rice. She wanted to have a shared meal that would "bring them together" without ruining her diet.

We went through the pantry items, veggies, and proteins she had bought for the week and the dinners she had planned. She settled on chicken fajitas and bulked up on the veggies (because she had stored a package of frozen fajita veggies for last-minute meals, she had plenty of bell peppers and onions to spare). And, for good measure, she included sliced mushrooms in the mix to enhance the "meatiness" of the dish. She garnished the veggies with a dollop of yogurt, some salsa, lime wedges, and fresh avocado slices. Her boyfriend loved it. Well done, Miss E!

Got some guests? Not to worry. My recipes can easily be doubled.

Yogurt Berry
French Toast
p. 18

CHAPTER TWO

Easy Breakfasts

Savory Eggs with Greens and Grains

MAKES 1 SERVING

ACTIVE TIME: *5 minutes* / **TOTAL TIME:** *15 minutes*

Barley and spinach make a great combo in this savory egg dish, but you can also swap them out for warmed oats and kale. Either way, it is a simple, savory breakfast (and a great way to use up any leftover grains). VEGETARIAN

½ cup water

¼ cup quick barley or rolled oats

1 loosely packed cup baby spinach or torn mature spinach

1 teaspoon extra-virgin olive oil

1 medium egg, beaten

⅛ teaspoon Italian seasoning

Pinch sea salt

1. In a small saucepan, combine the water and barley on medium heat. Bring to a boil and boil for 5 minutes.

2. Reduce the heat, cover, and continue to cook for another 2 to 3 minutes, until all the water is absorbed.

3. Turn off the heat. Add the spinach, cover the pan, and let sit for 3 minutes, or until the spinach has wilted and the barley is soft but still a little chewy (al dente).

4. Push the barley-spinach mixture to one side of the pan.

5. Add the oil to the empty half of the pan. Add the egg and scramble on medium-low heat for about 3 minutes, until the egg is set.

6. Season with the Italian seasoning and salt.

MAKE IT EASIER: Use leftover grains and skip steps 1 through 4. You can cook the egg and leftover grains together, then turn off the heat, add the spinach, and cover until the spinach is wilted.

———

Per serving: Calories: 247; Total fat: 10g; Carbohydrates: 30g; Fiber: 7g; Protein: 10g; Sodium: 232mg

Strawberry-Banana Smoothie

MAKES 1 SERVING

ACTIVE TIME: *5 minutes* / **TOTAL TIME:** *5 minutes*

This smoothie is made from the simplest ingredients. It's an easy way to pack in some tasty, nutrient-dense fruit and get plenty of protein and fiber to boot. **VEGETARIAN**

1 cup halved strawberries

½ **frozen banana, sliced** (if you have only fresh, just add a few ice cubes)

½ cup low-fat milk

¼ cup low-fat plain Greek yogurt

2 small pitted dates

1 teaspoon all-natural peanut butter

Combine the strawberries, banana, milk, yogurt, dates, and peanut butter in a high-speed blender. Blend until smooth and creamy.

HEALTHY HACK: Add a loose handful of spinach leaves to reap the nutritional benefits of those dark leafy greens. Spinach is so mild; once blended in this fruit-packed smoothie, you'll hardly taste it.

———

Per serving: Calories: 267; Total fat: 6g; Carbohydrates: 45g; Fiber: 6g; Protein: 13g; Sodium: 76mg

Yogurt Berry French Toast

MAKES 1 SERVING

ACTIVE TIME: *5 minutes* / **TOTAL TIME:** *5 minutes*

The addition of yogurt to the egg batter and as a final topping packs in good protein. And the cinnamon infuses a natural sweetness, so you won't be craving extra syrup or honey. If you've got fast-ripening fresh fruit, you can stew it in a small pot with a bit of water on the stove and serve it over your toast in place of the berries. **VEGETARIAN**

½ banana

1 medium egg

4 tablespoons low-fat plain Greek yogurt, divided

1 tablespoon low-fat milk

1 teaspoon honey

1 slice whole-grain bread, cut in half

Nonstick cooking spray

⅛ teaspoon ground cinnamon

¼ cup fresh or frozen berries

1. In a shallow bowl, mash the banana. Whisk in the egg, 2 tablespoons of yogurt, milk, and honey.

2. Using a fork or tongs, dunk the bread slices in the batter and turn to thoroughly coat both sides.

3. Coat a medium skillet with cooking spray and heat on medium for 30 seconds.

4. Add the coated bread slices to the pan and pour the remaining batter over the top (there will be extra spilling over the bread). Using a spatula, press the batter back onto the bread as it starts to set. Dust with the cinnamon and cook on medium for about 2 minutes on each side, until crisp and lightly browned.

5. Serve with the remaining 2 tablespoons of yogurt and fresh berries.

REUSE IT: Peel the remaining half of banana, tightly wrap it in plastic wrap, and store in the refrigerator. You can enjoy it with a tablespoon of peanut butter for a satisfying snack or in Banana-Pecan Oatmeal (page 19) the next day.

————

Per serving: Calories: 337; Total fat: 9g; Carbohydrates: 51g; Fiber: 6g; Protein: 17g; Sodium: 312mg

Banana-Pecan Oatmeal

MAKES 1 SERVING

ACTIVE TIME: *5 minutes* / **TOTAL TIME:** *15 minutes*

Get nutritious and delicious with this "banana bread" inspired oatmeal. It's a recipe you can make straight from your cupboard (sans the milk). Mix it, heat it, eat it—it's really that simple. VEGETARIAN

½ cup low-fat milk

½ banana, sliced

⅓ cup rolled oats

1 small pitted date, chopped

1 tablespoon chopped pecans

⅛ teaspoon sea salt

⅛ teaspoon vanilla extract or ground cinnamon

1. In a small saucepan, mix the milk, banana, oats, date, pecans, salt, and vanilla.

2. Cook on medium heat for about 3 minutes, until the mixture begins to boil.

3. Reduce the heat and simmer for 2 to 3 minutes.

4. Turn off the heat and cover for 5 minutes to fully thicken.

REUSE IT: Because you'll be using only half the banana, store the remaining half in a resealable plastic bag in the freezer for a refreshing smoothie the next day.

———

Per serving: Calories: 231; Total fat: 8g; Carbohydrates: 37g; Fiber: 5g; Protein: 5g; Sodium: 380mg

Apple-Cinnamon Oatmeal

MAKES 1 SERVING

ACTIVE TIME: *5 minutes* / **TOTAL TIME:** *10 minutes*

Skip the instant apple cinnamon oatmeal packet and make this instead. It's more satisfying and has less added sugar (and no artificial ingredients). **VEGETARIAN**

½ medium apple, chopped

⅔ cup water, divided

1 tablespoon dried cranberries

⅓ cup rolled oats

¼ teaspoon ground cinnamon, divided

¼ cup low-fat milk

1 tablespoon sliced almonds

1. In a small saucepan, combine the apple, ⅓ cup of water, and cranberries. Cover and cook on medium heat for 5 minutes, or until it reaches a slow boil and the apples soften.

2. Reduce the heat to medium-low, add the oats, remaining ⅓ cup of water, and ⅛ teaspoon of cinnamon. Cover and continue to cook for another 5 minutes.

3. Remove from the heat and transfer the mixture to a bowl. Add the milk, almonds, and remaining ⅛ teaspoon of cinnamon.

MAKE IT EASIER: Swap out the apple for any soft fresh fruit such as a pear or peach (or a rinsed, drained canned peach half) to skip step 1 and save 5 minutes. You can still use the cranberries—just add them in step 2.

Per serving: Calories: 252; Total fat: 6g; Carbohydrates: 36g; Fiber: 7g; Protein: 8g; Sodium: 36mg

Scrambled Egg in a Mug

MAKES 1 SERVING

ACTIVE TIME: *5 minutes* / **TOTAL TIME:** *5 minutes*

Who knew scrambled eggs could be even quicker, with no skillet or spatula to clean? This veggie egg scramble takes less than 2 minutes in a microwave, and the only thing you'll be washing is your mug and fork. VEGETARIAN

¼ cup chopped baby spinach

1 small tomato, chopped

1 medium egg

1 tablespoon low-fat milk

1 (1-ounce) **slice low-fat cheddar cheese**

1 slice multigrain bread, toasted

1 teaspoon butter or extra-virgin olive oil

1. Put the spinach and tomato in a microwave-safe mug.

2. Crack the egg on top and add the milk. Mix well with a fork.

3. Microwave for 90 seconds, or until the egg has firmed.

4. Stir in the cheese—it should melt in the mug with the warm egg combo.

5. Serve on the toast with a little pat of butter or a drizzle of oil.

HEALTHY HACK: Skip the cheese and top with a spoonful of salsa for a zesty scrambled egg.

———

Per serving: Calories: 237; Total fat: 12g; Carbohydrates: 16g; Fiber: 3g; Protein: 17g; Sodium: 409mg

Yogurt Berry Parfait

MAKES 1 SERVING
ACTIVE TIME: *5 minutes* / **TOTAL TIME:** *5 minutes*

You can make this simple, tasty breakfast treat in minutes. Style it up in alternating layers or simply top your yogurt base with fresh fruit and my simple DIY muesli. VEGETARIAN

¼ cup rolled oats

1 tablespoon dried cranberries

1 tablespoon sliced almonds

1 cup nonfat plain Greek yogurt
(or ½ cup nonfat plain yogurt plus ½ cup nonfat ricotta)

Juice of 1 lemon (optional)

1 teaspoon honey

¾ cup fresh or frozen berries

1. In a small bowl, combine the oats, cranberries, and almonds.

2. In another small bowl, mix the yogurt, lemon juice (if using), and honey.

3. In a small bowl or jar, layer the honey-yogurt mixture, berries, and muesli.

MAKE IT EASIER: Swap the DIY muesli for ¼ cup of your favorite chopped nuts.

Per serving: Calories: 375; Total fat: 6g; Carbohydrates: 52g; Fiber: 6g; Protein: 30g; Sodium: 101mg

Egg in a Hole

MAKES 1 SERVING

ACTIVE TIME: *5 minutes* / **TOTAL TIME:** *5 minutes*

Prepare this unique twist on an egg sandwich for a one-skillet meal. You'll need a juice glass with a 3-inch rim to cut the hole in your bread (or use a cookie cutter). VEGETARIAN

1 slice multigrain bread

Nonstick cooking spray

1 tablespoon chopped scallion greens (or up to ¼ cup chopped leftover cooked veggies)

1 medium egg

1 (1-ounce) slice low-fat cheddar or provolone cheese

1 medium tomato, sliced

1 cup baby spinach

1. Use the rim of a small glass to cut a hole in the center of the bread.

2. Lightly coat a nonstick skillet with cooking spray and place the bread in the pan, with the removed bread circle next to it. Heat on medium-low for 30 seconds.

3. Add the scallions to the hole in the bread.

4. Crack an egg on top, directly over the scallions. If it spills over the hole, not to worry. The egg will poke through on the other side.

5. Cook for about 2 minutes, until the egg starts to set and the underside of the bread has browned. Remove the bread circle and set aside.

6. Flip the bread and egg and continue to cook for another 2 minutes, or until the egg white is fully set and the bread is completely toasted. Add the cheese on top, turn off the heat, and cover the pan for 1 minute to let the cheese melt.

7. Top the toast and egg with a slice of tomato and the bread circle (or you can choose to eat that first). Serve over a pile of spinach greens and the remaining tomato slices. Use a fork and knife and enjoy!

REUSE IT: Leftover veggies are great for this dish because they cook into the egg, packing some fiber and B vitamins into this meal.

———

Per serving: Calories: 294; Total fat: 13g; Carbohydrates: 25g; Fiber: 5g; Protein: 20g; Sodium: 485mg

Ricotta with Fresh Berries

MAKES 1 SERVING

ACTIVE TIME: *5 minutes* / **TOTAL TIME:** *5 minutes*

This ricotta dish comes together quickly—no cooking necessary. Use whatever kind of berries you like. If you use thawed frozen berries, you'll also get a delightfully sweet berry juice to mix in. **VEGETARIAN**

½ **cup nonfat ricotta cheese**

1 **teaspoon honey** (optional)

½ **cup fresh or frozen** (thawed) **berries**

1 **tablespoon sliced almonds**

1. Put the ricotta in a small bowl and drizzle with the honey (if using).
2. Add the berries.
3. Sprinkle the almonds on top.

HEALTHY HACK: To get some gut-friendly probiotics, swap half the ricotta for low-fat plain Greek yogurt and mix until well combined.

———

Per serving: Calories: 271; Total fat: 14g; Carbohydrates: 22g; Fiber: 3g; Protein: 16g; Sodium: 130mg

Grilled Peach and Ricotta Toast

MAKES 1 SERVING

ACTIVE TIME: *5 minutes* / **TOTAL TIME:** *10 minutes*

This breakfast dish has a French toast appeal, but it's actually egg-free. Caramelized peaches leave a sweet-tangy juice that infuses into the bread as it toasts in the pan for a one-skillet breakfast that's certainly a treat! VEGETARIAN

Nonstick cooking spray

1 medium ripe peach, pitted and sliced (or 2 canned peach halves, drained and sliced)

1 loosely packed cup baby spinach

1 slice whole-grain bread

¼ cup nonfat ricotta cheese

Ground cinnamon (optional)

1. Coat a medium skillet with cooking spray and heat on medium for 30 seconds.

2. Add the peaches and cook for 5 minutes.

3. Add the spinach and stir into the peaches. With a spatula, push the combo to one side of the pan.

4. Spray one side of the bread with cooking spray and place that side in the empty space in the pan.

5. Toast the bread in the pan for 2 to 3 minutes, then flip and cook for another 2 to 3 minutes, until the bread is fully toasted, the spinach is wilted, and the peaches have caramelized.

6. Remove the toast, spread evenly with the ricotta, and spoon the peach and spinach mixture on top. Sprinkle with cinnamon (if using).

MAKE IT EASIER: Toast your bread, smear on the ricotta, and top with spinach and fresh peaches for an open-faced sandwich combo you can eat with a fork. This no-cook combo is a breeze.

Per serving: Calories: 245; Total fat: 8g; Carbohydrates: 33g; Fiber: 5g; Protein: 13g; Sodium: 184mg

Herbed Tuna
Salad Sandwich
p. 33

Chicken Salad Pita

MAKES 1 SERVING

ACTIVE TIME: *10 minutes* / **TOTAL TIME:** *10 minutes*

Store-bought reduced-fat mayo can be hit and miss in terms of flavor. Instead, you can whip up a simple, healthy DIY seasoned spread made with Greek yogurt. Then you can use a generous dollop without worrying about excess fat or calories.

FOR THE SEASONED YOGURT MAYO

½ cup low-fat plain Greek yogurt

1 tablespoon extra-virgin olive oil

1 to 2 tablespoons low-fat milk

2 teaspoons Dijon mustard

2 teaspoons honey

⅛ teaspoon sea salt

FOR THE CHICKEN SALAD PITA

4 ounces cooked chicken breast, chopped

¼ cup chopped celery

¼ cup chopped cucumber or zucchini

1 tablespoon dried cranberries

Freshly ground black pepper or lemon pepper seasoning (optional)

½ whole-wheat pita

1. To make the seasoned yogurt mayo, in a small bowl, combine the yogurt, oil, milk, mustard, honey, and salt and mix well.

2. To make the chicken salad, in a medium bowl, toss together the chicken, celery, cucumber, and cranberries.

3. Gently mix in 2 tablespoons of the seasoned yogurt mixture until well combined.

4. Season with pepper (if using) to taste. Scoop into the pita.

REUSE IT: Save the remaining seasoned yogurt mayo in a small jar or other airtight container in the refrigerator for up to a week. It is used in both the Herbed Tuna Salad Sandwich (page 33) and Creamy Broccoli Salad (page 41).

———

Per serving: Calories: 346; Total fat: 8g; Carbohydrates: 28g; Fiber: 3g; Protein: 40g; Sodium: 474mg

Saucy Bean Burrito Bowl

MAKES 2 SERVINGS

ACTIVE TIME: *15 minutes* / **TOTAL TIME:** *30 minutes*

Caramelized onions add so much flavor to this bean burrito, which is packed with colorful veggies to boot. I recommend you eat this one using a fork and knife—it's good and messy! VEGETARIAN

1 teaspoon extra-virgin olive oil

¼ cup chopped onion

¼ cup chopped bell pepper (any color)

Pinch sea salt

2 to 4 teaspoons water

Nonstick cooking spray (optional)

1 (9-inch) whole-wheat tortilla

½ cup canned low-sodium black beans

¼ cup frozen corn

¼ cup low-sodium marinara sauce (or ¼ cup canned low-sodium crushed tomatoes plus pinch Tuscan seasoning)

1 tablespoon low-fat plain Greek yogurt

1 sprig fresh cilantro (optional)

Sriracha

1. Heat the oil in a medium skillet on medium-high heat for 30 seconds. Add the onion, bell pepper, and salt, reduce the heat to medium-low, and cook for 10 minutes, stirring to prevent sticking. Add a little water as needed to prevent overbrowning.

2. Cover and cook for another 5 minutes, or until the onion is translucent and the bell pepper is soft.

3. While the veggies are cooking, if desired, coat a 6-inch skillet with cooking spray and heat the tortilla with the edges folded up for about 2 minutes, until crisp and formed into a loose bowl shape.

4. Add the beans, corn, and marinara to the onion and bell pepper mixture, cover, and cook for about 5 minutes, until heated through.

5. Place the tortilla on a large plate and fill it with the saucy bean and veggie mixture.

6. Top with yogurt and garnish with cilantro (if using). Serve with sriracha to taste.

REUSE IT: Transfer the remaining portion to an airtight container and store in the refrigerator for up to 2 days. Reheat in a skillet to re-crisp the tortilla.

———

Per serving: Calories: 300; Total fat: 9g; Carbohydrates: 45g; Fiber: 13g; Protein: 15g; Sodium: 619mg

Chicken Gyro with Bell Peppers and Onions

MAKES 1 SERVING
ACTIVE TIME: *10 minutes* / **TOTAL TIME:** *20 minutes*

Sautéed peppers and onions and a creamy dill-seasoned yogurt make for a savory and refreshing take on the traditional gyro. This dish is a perfect use for leftover chicken, although you can always purchase cooked chicken strips at the grocery store.

FOR THE YOGURT-DILL DRESSING

¼ cup low-fat plain Greek yogurt

¼ cup chopped cucumber

1 teaspoon chopped fresh dill or
¼ teaspoon dried dill

1 teaspoon extra-virgin olive oil

¼ teaspoon garlic powder

FOR THE GYRO

1 teaspoon extra-virgin olive oil

¼ cup chopped onion

¼ cup chopped bell pepper (any color)

Pinch sea salt

2 to 4 teaspoons water

4 ounces cooked chicken breast, cut into strips

½ whole-wheat pita

1. To make the yogurt-dill dressing, combine the yogurt, cucumber, dill, oil, and garlic powder in a medium bowl and mix until well combined. Set aside.

2. To make the gyro, heat the oil in a medium skillet on medium-high heat for 30 seconds. Add the onion, bell pepper, and salt, reduce the heat to medium-low, and cook for 10 minutes, stirring to prevent sticking. Add a little water as needed to prevent overbrowning.

3. Cover and cook for another 5 minutes, or until the onion is translucent and the bell pepper is soft.

4. Mix the chicken into the yogurt-dill dressing.

5. Fill the pita with the chicken mixture and sautéed veggies.

HEALTHY HACK: For even more fiber, pack a handful of leafy greens into the pita before adding the chicken and veggies.

———

Per serving: Calories: 349; Total fat: 14g; Carbohydrates: 23g; Fiber: 3g; Protein: 33g; Sodium: 344mg

Tuna Niçoise Salad

MAKES 1 SERVING

ACTIVE TIME: *10 minutes* / **TOTAL TIME:** *10 minutes*

This salad packs in veggies, protein, and plenty of flavor. And if you have tuna salad on hand, it's a perfect way to leverage those leftovers in a whole new way!

FOR THE TUNA SALAD

1 cup baby spinach

3 ounces canned wild-caught tuna, drained, or leftover Herbed Tuna Salad (page 33)

½ cup green beans, cooked and cooled

1 small potato, cooked and sliced, or 3 baby potatoes, cooked and halved

1 hard-boiled egg, cut into quarters

2 medium pitted green olives or 2 teaspoons capers

FOR THE DRESSING

Juice of 1 lemon or 2 teaspoons balsamic vinegar

1 tablespoon grated Parmesan cheese

2 teaspoons extra-virgin olive oil

½ teaspoon Dijon mustard

1. To make the tuna salad, put the spinach in a medium bowl.

2. Layer on the tuna, green beans, potato, egg, and olives.

3. To make the dressing, in a small bowl, whisk together the lemon juice, Parmesan, oil, and Dijon.

4. Drizzle the dressing on the salad and toss until the spinach is well coated.

REUSE IT: If you've got leftover canned tuna, transfer it to an airtight container and store in the refrigerator for up to 3 days. You can add it to scrambled eggs for a protein-packed breakfast or save it for a tuna sandwich.

———

Per serving: Calories: 317; Total fat: 17g; Carbohydrates: 27g; Fiber: 5g; Protein: 19g; Sodium: 558mg

Healthy Cobb Salad

MAKES 1 SERVING

ACTIVE TIME: *10 minutes* / **TOTAL TIME:** *10 minutes*

This hearty Cobb salad packs in plenty of protein! I've kept it traditional but made it a bit leaner with a few slight adjustments, such as turkey bacon instead of regular bacon. It's so tasty and satisfying, you won't even miss the blue cheese.

Nonstick cooking spray

1 slice turkey bacon

1 cup chopped romaine lettuce

1 hard-boiled egg, chopped

3 ounces cooked chicken breast, chopped

1 medium tomato, chopped

½ medium avocado, sliced, or ½ cup canned low-sodium chickpeas

2 teaspoons extra-virgin olive oil

1 teaspoon balsamic vinegar

1. Spray a small skillet with cooking spray and heat on medium heat for 30 seconds. Add the turkey bacon and cook for about 4 minutes each side, until crisp. Let cool, then crumble.

2. Put the lettuce in a medium bowl.

3. Layer on the bacon, egg, chicken, tomato, and avocado.

4. Add the oil and vinegar. Toss the salad until well combined.

MAKE IT EASIER: Instead of the turkey bacon, you can use 2 ounces leftover Braised Tofu (page 47) and just skip step 1.

———

Per serving: Calories: 314; Total fat: 23g; Carbohydrates: 11g; Fiber: 5g; Protein: 19g; Sodium: 264mg

Herbed Tuna Salad Sandwich

MAKES 1 SERVING

ACTIVE TIME: *10 minutes* / **TOTAL TIME:** *10 minutes*

Straight from the can, tuna is an easy protein choice. You can make it deliciously creamy using my DIY Seasoned Yogurt Mayo (page 28).

1 (5-ounce) **can wild-caught tuna, drained**

1 **medium tomato, chopped**

¼ cup **chopped scallion greens**

2 tablespoons **Seasoned Yogurt Mayo**
(page 28)

2 **medium pitted green olives or**
2 **teaspoons capers, chopped**

¼ **teaspoon garlic powder**

⅛ **teaspoon lemon pepper seasoning**

2 slices **whole-grain bread**

1 **romaine lettuce leaf**

1. Put the tuna in a medium bowl and flake it with a fork.

2. Add the tomato, scallions, yogurt mayo, olives, garlic powder, and lemon pepper. Mix until well combined.

3. Scoop half the tuna salad onto one slice of bread.

4. Add the lettuce leaf and top it with the remaining slice of bread.

REUSE IT: Store the leftover tuna salad in an airtight container in the refrigerator for up to 2 days. You can use it to make Tuna Niçoise Salad (page 31).

Per serving: Calories: 343; Total fat: 10g; Carbohydrates: 37g; Fiber: 7g; Protein: 27g; Sodium: 462mg

Egg Salad Sandwich

MAKES 1 SERVING

ACTIVE TIME: *5 minutes* / **TOTAL TIME:** *5 minutes*

This simple recipe swaps out the mayonnaise used in traditional egg salad to keep it light and healthy. Instead, it calls for my easy DIY Seasoned Yogurt Mayo (page 28). VEGETARIAN

2 tablespoons Seasoned Yogurt Mayo (page 28)

2 teaspoons Dijon mustard

¼ teaspoon garlic powder

2 teaspoons chopped scallion greens

2 hard-boiled eggs, chopped

2 slices whole-grain bread

1 crisp romaine lettuce leaf

1 medium tomato, sliced

1. In a small bowl, whisk together the seasoned yogurt mayo, Dijon, and garlic powder. Fold in the scallions.

2. Stir in the chopped egg until well incorporated.

3. Scoop the egg mixture onto one slice of bread. Top with the lettuce and tomato and the remaining slice of bread.

MAKE IT EASIER: Swap the DIY seasoned yogurt mayo for 1 tablespoon reduced-fat mayo plus 1 tablespoon low-fat plain Greek yogurt.

———————

Per serving: Calories: 335; Total fat: 13g; Carbohydrates: 34g; Fiber: 7g; Protein: 22g; Sodium: 681mg

Grilled Veggie Sandwich Wrap

MAKES 1 SERVING

ACTIVE TIME: *10 minutes* / **TOTAL TIME:** *20 minutes*

Enjoy fresh grilled veggies, served conveniently with hummus in a simple wrap. This vegan dish is a perfect way to get in plenty of veggie protein and keep you satisfied. VEGAN

1 teaspoon extra-virgin olive oil

¼ cup chopped onion

¼ cup chopped bell pepper (any color)

Pinch sea salt

2 to 4 teaspoons water

1 small zucchini, chopped

1 cup baby spinach

1 (8-inch) whole-wheat tortilla

2 tablespoons hummus

1. Heat the oil in a medium skillet on medium-high heat for 30 seconds. Add the onion, bell pepper, and salt, reduce the heat to medium, and cook for 5 to 7 minutes, stirring to prevent sticking. Add water as needed to prevent sticking.

2. Add the zucchini, cover, and cook for 5 minutes, or until the onion and bell pepper are soft.

3. Turn off the heat, add the spinach, and cover for 5 minutes to wilt the spinach and soften the zucchini.

4. Push the veggie mixture to one side of the pan. Fold the tortilla and place it in the empty side of the pan. Heat on low until warmed, about 2 minutes.

5. Transfer the tortilla to a plate. Spread the hummus on the tortilla, top with the grilled veggies, and roll into a wrap.

REUSE IT: Store the remaining raw onion and bell pepper in an airtight container in the refrigerator for up to 1 week. You can slice them ahead of time to have them prepped for my Simple Veggie Stir-Fry (page 36).

Per serving: Calories: 300; Total fat: 11g; Carbohydrates: 42g; Fiber: 9g; Protein: 10g; Sodium: 482mg

Simple Veggie Stir-Fry

MAKES 1 SERVING

ACTIVE TIME: *5 minutes* / **TOTAL TIME:** *15 minutes*

A simple stir-fry that uses both fresh and frozen veggies can make for a flavorful midday meal. Using instant brown rice will cut your time in half, and you can prepare your veggies while the rice is cooking. **VEGAN**

2 teaspoons extra-virgin olive oil

1 teaspoon peeled minced fresh ginger or ½ teaspoon ground ginger

1 teaspoon soy sauce

½ teaspoon garlic powder

⅛ teaspoon sea salt

¼ cup chopped onion

¼ cup chopped bell pepper (any color)

2 to 4 teaspoons water

1 cup frozen peas and carrots

½ cup cooked brown rice

1. Heat the oil, ginger, soy sauce, garlic powder, and salt in a medium skillet on medium-high heat for 30 seconds.

2. Reduce the heat to medium and stir in the onion and bell pepper. Cook for about 7 minutes, stirring occasionally, until softened. Add water as needed to prevent sticking.

3. Add the peas and carrots. Reduce the heat to low and continue to cook for 5 minutes, or until heated through.

4. Stir in the cooked rice.

HEALTHY HACK: To get in some satisfying vegetable protein, add ½ cup canned low-sodium chickpeas.

Per serving: Calories: 212; Total fat: 10g; Carbohydrates: 29g; Fiber: 6g; Protein: 6g; Sodium: 542mg

Spinach and Peach Salad with Avocado

MAKES 1 SERVING

ACTIVE TIME: *10 minutes* / **TOTAL TIME:** *10 minutes*

A juicy, ripe peach and the creaminess of avocado make this spinach salad a refreshing, tasty choice. The tangy dressing pulls it all together. It's a simple way to pack a salad with plenty of antioxidant potential, and it's satisfying, too! VEGETARIAN

FOR THE DRESSING

2 teaspoons extra-virgin olive oil

2 teaspoons apple cider vinegar

¼ teaspoon Dijon mustard

¼ teaspoon honey

FOR THE SALAD

1 cup baby spinach

1 medium ripe peach, pitted and sliced

½ medium avocado, cubed

1 ounce burrata or nonfat ricotta cheese

1 tablespoon chopped walnuts

1. To make the dressing, in a small bowl, whisk together the oil, vinegar, Dijon, and honey until well combined.

2. In a serving bowl, toss the spinach, peaches, and avocado. Pull off bits of the burrata and scatter them on top.

3. Drizzle the dressing on the salad and toss until well coated. Sprinkle the walnuts on top.

REUSE IT: Wrap the remaining avocado half tightly in plastic wrap, pit intact. Refrigerate for up to 2 days.

———

Per serving: Calories: 406; Total fat: 32g; Carbohydrates: 24g; Fiber: 8g; Protein: 10g; Sodium: 146mg

Chickpea and Farro Salad

MAKES 1 SERVING

ACTIVE TIME: *5 minutes* / **TOTAL TIME:** *15 minutes*

This satisfying combo is another mostly "straight from the cupboard" meal. If you've never had farro, I think you'll enjoy its nutty flavor and chewy texture. With both farro and chickpeas, this salad provides a whopping dose of protein, fiber, and other essential nutrients. VEGETARIAN

¼ cup instant farro or barley

2 teaspoons extra-virgin olive oil

2 tablespoons chopped scallion greens

½ cup canned low-sodium chickpeas

⅛ teaspoon garlic powder

Tiny pinch salt

¼ cup canned low-sodium diced tomato, drained, or 1 small tomato, sliced

3 leaves fresh basil, chopped or thinly sliced or ¼ teaspoon dried basil

1 tablespoon grated Parmesan cheese

1. Prepare the farro according to package instructions.

2. Heat the oil in a small saucepan on medium heat for 30 seconds. Add the scallions and cook for 2 minutes, or until slightly browned. Mix in the chickpeas, garlic powder, and salt. Turn off the heat and cover to warm the chickpeas through.

3. Transfer the farro and chickpea mixture to a bowl and add the tomatoes, basil, and Parmesan.

HEALTHY HACK: Swap the Parmesan for 1 tablespoon sliced almonds and serve over a bed of leafy greens.

Per serving: Calories: 398; Total fat: 14g; Carbohydrates: 58g; Fiber: 13g; Protein: 15g; Sodium: 369mg

Chickpea-Avocado Wrap

MAKES 1 SERVING

ACTIVE TIME: *5 minutes* / **TOTAL TIME:** *5 minutes*

Mashed chickpeas, seasonings, and spices plus creamy avocado make this simple wrap a tasty treat! It also boasts plenty of protein and fiber. VEGAN

½ cup canned low-sodium chickpeas

1 small tomato, diced

1 tablespoon chopped scallion greens

1 teaspoon Dijon mustard

¼ teaspoon extra-virgin olive oil

⅛ teaspoon lemon pepper seasoning or your favorite spice blend

1 (8-inch) whole-wheat tortilla

2 tablespoons hummus

¼ avocado, sliced

¼ cup baby spinach

Nonstick cooking spray

1. In a medium bowl, mash the chickpeas with a fork. Mix in the tomato, scallions, Dijon, oil, and lemon pepper.

2. Spread the tortilla evenly with the hummus.

3. Add the chickpea mixture. Place the avocado slices in the center and layer with the spinach leaves. Roll into a wrap.

4. Coat a nonstick skillet with cooking spray and heat on medium for 30 seconds. Place the wrap in the pan and toast for 1 to 2 minutes on each side, until golden and crisp.

REUSE IT: Wrap the remainder of the avocado tightly in plastic wrap, including the pit, and refrigerate for up to 2 days. You can make a simple guacamole by mashing the avocado with lemon juice, garlic powder, and a pinch of sea salt—it's perfect to pair with carrot sticks for a satisfying snack.

Per serving: Calories: 388; Total fat: 16g; Carbohydrates: 51g; Fiber: 15g; Protein: 14g; Sodium: 568mg

Braised Tofu "BLT"

MAKES 1 SERVING

ACTIVE TIME: *5 minutes* / **TOTAL TIME:** *10 minutes*

Who knew braised tofu could be so full of flavor? In fact, it's so savory, it makes a great alternative to the bacon in a BLT. VEGETARIAN

1 tablespoon water, divided

1 teaspoon low-sodium soy sauce

1 teaspoon peeled minced fresh ginger

1 teaspoon honey

⅛ teaspoon garlic powder

1 teaspoon extra-virgin olive oil

3½ ounces firm tofu, cut into ¼-inch slices

2 tablespoons Seasoned Yogurt Mayo (page 28) or 1 tablespoon reduced-fat mayonnaise

2 slices whole-grain bread, toasted

1 or 2 romaine lettuce leaves

1 small tomato, sliced

1. In a small bowl, whisk together 1 tablespoon of water, the soy sauce, ginger, honey, and garlic powder.

2. Heat the oil in a small skillet on medium heat for 30 seconds. Add the tofu slices and cook for 3 to 4 minutes on each side, until browned.

3. Pour the soy mixture over the tofu and cook for about 1 minute, until all the liquid is absorbed.

4. Spread the yogurt mayo evenly on both slices of toast. Layer with the braised tofu, lettuce, and tomato and sandwich together.

HEALTHY HACK: For a lower-carb and lower-sodium version, serve the sandwich open-face on just one slice of whole-grain toast.

————

Per serving: Calories: 389; Total fat: 19g; Carbohydrates: 34g; Fiber: 8g; Protein: 26g; Sodium: 537mg

Creamy Broccoli Salad

MAKES 2 SERVINGS

ACTIVE TIME: *10 minutes* / **TOTAL TIME:** *10 minutes*

This raw broccoli salad is made with a yogurt-based mayo for a meal with plenty of protein and gut-friendly probiotics.

Nonstick cooking spray

2 slices lean turkey bacon

1½ cups small broccoli florets

1 cup baby spinach

¼ cup chopped scallion greens

2 tablespoons dried cranberries

2 tablespoons sliced almonds

¾ cup Seasoned Yogurt Mayo (page 28)

1 tablespoon balsamic vinegar (optional)

1. Spray a small skillet with cooking spray and heat on medium heat for 30 seconds. Add the turkey bacon and cook for 4 minutes on each side, or until crisp. Let cool, then crumble.

2. In a large bowl, toss together the broccoli, spinach, scallions, cranberries, almonds, and turkey bacon.

3. Add the yogurt mayo and toss well to thoroughly coat. If you'd like to make the salad a little tangier, mix in the balsamic vinegar.

REUSE IT: Transfer half the salad to an airtight container and refrigerate for up to 4 days.

Per serving: Calories: 300; Total fat: 13g; Carbohydrates: 35g; Fiber: 4g; Protein: 14g; Sodium: 473mg

Grilled Pear and Cheese Sandwich

MAKES 1 SERVING

ACTIVE TIME: *10 minutes* / **TOTAL TIME:** *10 minutes*

Kick your grilled cheese up a notch with a two-cheese blend and fresh pear slices. It's a sweet and savory combo that's always appealing. VEGETARIAN

¼ cup nonfat ricotta cheese

2 slices whole-grain bread

1 teaspoon extra-virgin olive oil

½ ounce (½ single slice) cheddar cheese

1 ripe pear, cored and sliced

Nonstick cooking spray (optional)

1. Spread the ricotta evenly on both slices of bread.

2. Heat the oil in a medium skillet on medium heat for 30 seconds, swirling the pan to coat the entire bottom. Add the bread, ricotta-side up.

3. Top one slice with the cheddar cheese and pear and heat for 3 to 4 minutes, until the bottoms of the bread have browned.

4. Assemble into a sandwich. If you like, lightly spritz the sandwich with cooking spray.

HEALTHY HACK: To get in some veggies, add a loose handful of baby spinach on top of the pear layer in step 3.

———

Per serving: Calories: 298; Total fat: 13g; Carbohydrates: 27g; Fiber: 4g; Protein: 18g; Sodium: 395mg

Shakshuka
with Broccoli
p. 56

CHAPTER FOUR

Vegetable Mains

Cream of Broccoli with Corn and Sausage

MAKES 2 SERVINGS

ACTIVE TIME: *10 minutes* / **TOTAL TIME:** *25 minutes*

This cream of broccoli soup is made without any dairy. The secret to its creaminess is the starchy corn and avocado.

2 teaspoons extra-virgin olive oil

1½ cups broccoli florets

¾ cup corn

¼ cup finely chopped onion or scallion greens

¼ cup finely chopped carrot

⅛ teaspoon garlic powder

2 cups low-sodium chicken broth

2 tablespoons all-purpose flour

4 precooked turkey sausage breakfast links

½ medium avocado

Freshly ground black pepper

1. Heat the oil in a small saucepan on medium heat for 30 seconds.

2. Add the broccoli, corn, onion, carrot, and garlic powder and cook, stirring occasionally, for 5 to 7 minutes, until the onion is translucent.

3. Add the broth and flour and cook, stirring constantly, until no lumps remain, about 5 minutes.

4. Cover and continue to cook for 7 minutes, or until the carrot and broccoli soften.

5. Meanwhile, heat the sausages in the microwave according to package instructions.

6. Transfer two-thirds of the broccoli mixture to a blender, add the avocado, and process until well pureed.

7. Divide the pureed blend evenly between a storage container and a bowl. Divide the remaining skillet mixture between the container and bowl. Slice and divide the sausages between the two. Seal the storage container and refrigerate for up to 2 days.

8. Season the bowl of soup with pepper to taste.

REUSE IT: Seal the remaining half of avocado, pit intact, tightly in plastic wrap and store in the refrigerator for up to 2 days or in the freezer for up to 6 months.

———

Per serving: Calories: 307; Total fat: 16g; Carbohydrates: 30g; Fiber: 7g; Protein: 15g; Sodium: 453mg

Braised Tofu with Zucchini and Carrots

MAKES 1 SERVING

ACTIVE TIME: *5 minutes* / **TOTAL TIME:** *20 minutes*

Braising tofu keeps it firm but prevents it from drying out while infusing it with flavor. It's one my favorite ways to enjoy this protein. VEGETARIAN

1 tablespoon low-sodium soy sauce

1 tablespoon water, plus ¼ cup

1 teaspoon honey

1 teaspoon peeled minced fresh ginger

⅛ teaspoon garlic powder

1 teaspoon extra-virgin olive oil

3 ounces firm tofu, drained, patted dry, and cubed

1 small zucchini, chopped

¼ cup chopped carrot

½ cup cooked brown rice

1. In a small bowl, whisk together the soy sauce, 1 tablespoon of water, honey, ginger, and garlic powder. Set aside.

2. Heat the oil in a medium skillet on medium heat for 30 seconds. Cook the tofu for 3 to 4 minutes on each side, until golden.

3. Pour the sauce over the tofu and simmer for 1 to 2 minutes.

4. Transfer the tofu to a plate. Add the zucchini, carrot, and remaining ¼ cup of water to the skillet. Cover and cook for 7 to 8 minutes, until the veggies are soft.

5. Serve the tofu and veggies over the prepared rice.

MAKE IT EASIER: Instead of fresh zucchini and carrots, use about 1 cup of a blend of your favorite frozen mixed veggies.

Per serving: Calories: 295; Total fat: 13g; Carbohydrates: 30g; Fiber: 5g; Protein: 19g; Sodium: 236mg

Hearty Grain Bowl with Seasoned Black Beans

MAKES 2 SERVINGS

ACTIVE TIME: *5 minutes* / **TOTAL TIME:** *20 minutes*

This bowl can be customized for your favorite whole grains with any combo of veggies you have on hand. But for this recipe, we'll use brown rice with carrots and celery—two common staples that hold up quite well in the refrigerator. VEGAN

¾ cup chopped carrot

¾ cup chopped celery

2 teaspoons extra-virgin olive oil

⅛ teaspoon garlic powder

⅛ teaspoon Tuscan seasoning or Italian seasoning

Pinch sea salt

1 (15-ounce) **can low-sodium black beans, drained and rinsed**

1 cup cooked brown rice

4 tablespoons salsa, divided

1. Put the carrots and celery in a microwave-safe bowl, pour in about ¼ inch of water, cover, and microwave for 4 minutes. Drain and set aside.

2. Meanwhile, in a medium skillet, heat the oil with the garlic, Tuscan seasoning, and salt on medium heat for 30 seconds.

3. Stir in the beans and continue to heat for 2 minutes, or until the beans are warmed. Push the beans to one side, add the steamed carrots and celery to the empty side, and cook for 2 minutes, or until lightly toasted.

4. Divide the rice, seasoned beans, and celery-carrot mixture evenly between a bowl and an airtight container so you can store your leftovers. Garnish each serving with 2 tablespoons of salsa.

5. Seal the container with the leftovers and refrigerate for up to 2 days.

MAKE IT EASIER: Swap the raw carrots and celery for 1½ cup frozen mixed veggies and skip step 1.

Per serving: Calories: 350; Total fat: 6g; Carbohydrates: 62g; Fiber: 17g; Protein: 14g; Sodium: 474mg

Mini Skillet Frittata

MAKES 2 SERVINGS

ACTIVE TIME: *10 minutes* / **TOTAL TIME:** *30 minutes*

Why not make a double frittata so you can eat half and save the rest for another meal? Serve with a side salad or a cup of fresh fruit. VEGETARIAN

2 teaspoons extra-virgin olive oil	1 cup mixed frozen veggies
2 tablespoons chopped scallion greens	4 medium eggs
⅛ teaspoon garlic powder	⅓ cup low-fat milk
⅛ teaspoon Tuscan seasoning or Italian seasoning	¼ cup nonfat ricotta cheese
Pinch sea salt	¼ cup grated Parmesan cheese

1. Preheat the oven to 350°F.

2. Heat the oil in a small oven-safe nonstick skillet with the scallions, garlic powder, Tuscan seasoning, and salt on medium heat for 30 seconds.

3. Add the veggies and sauté for 5 minutes, or until warmed through.

4. In a medium bowl, whisk together the eggs, milk, and ricotta, then stir in the Parmesan.

5. Add the eggs to the veggie mixture and heat for 2 minutes, or until the eggs just start to set on the outer edges.

6. Transfer to the oven and bake for 12 to 14 minutes, until fluffy and firm, with the center just a little jiggly. The frittata will continue to cook from the heat of the pan once removed from the oven. Cut the frittata in half and store one portion in an airtight container in the refrigerator for up to 4 days, then reheat in a 350°F oven for 10 minutes or in a microwave for 30 to 40 seconds.

MAKE IT EASIER: You can easily prepare this recipe in a muffin tin for snack-size mini frittatas. Line 4 cups of a muffin tin with cupcake liners and a light coat of cooking spray in each. Follow steps 1 through 4 above. Divide the sautéed veggies equally among the cups, then pour in an equal amount of the egg mixture. Bake for about 15 minutes, until fluffy and firm, with a slightly jiggly center. Let the mini frittatas cool, then enjoy or store individually in the refrigerator.

Per serving: Calories: 335; Total fat: 21g; Carbohydrates: 15g; Fiber: 2g; Protein: 21g; Sodium: 471mg

Veggie Stuffed Bell Pepper with Mushrooms and Ricotta

MAKES 2 SERVINGS

ACTIVE TIME: *10 minutes* / **TOTAL TIME:** *30 minutes*

This savory stuffed bell pepper smells like a pizza fresh out of the oven. It just oozes with filling, so you'll be glad to have some bread to soak up the sauce. **VEGETARIAN**

Nonstick cooking spray

2 large bell peppers (any color)

¼ cup nonfat ricotta cheese

¼ cup frozen peas

½ teaspoon garlic powder, divided

½ teaspoon Tuscan seasoning
(or ½ teaspoon Italian seasoning plus pinch red pepper flakes), **divided**

1 teaspoon extra-virgin olive oil

½ cup sliced mushrooms

¼ cup chopped scallion greens

¼ cup chopped celery

½ cup plus 2 tablespoons canned low-sodium chickpeas, divided

4 tablespoons low-sodium marinara sauce, divided

2 tablespoons grated Parmesan cheese, divided

½ medium pita

1. Preheat the oven to 425ºF. Line a rimmed baking sheet with aluminum foil. Lightly coat the foil with cooking spray.

2. Slice the tops off the bell peppers and remove the ribs and seeds inside.

3. In a small bowl, combine the ricotta, peas, ¼ teaspoon of garlic powder, and ¼ teaspoon of Tuscan seasoning.

4. Fill each bell pepper with an equal amount of the ricotta mixture. Place on the prepared baking sheet and bake for about 10 minutes, while you prepare the veggies.

5. Meanwhile, heat the oil in a medium skillet on medium heat for 30 seconds. Add the mushrooms, scallions, celery, and remaining ¼ teaspoon of garlic powder and cook, stirring occasionally, for 5 minutes.

6. Reduce the heat to low, cover, and continue to heat for another 5 minutes, or until the celery is just tender. Turn off the heat and stir in ½ cup of chickpeas.

7. Remove the baking sheet from the oven and fill each bell pepper with an equal amount of the veggie mixture. Top each with 2 tablespoons of marinara, 1 tablespoon of the remaining chickpeas, and 1 tablespoon of Parmesan cheese.

8. Return to the oven and bake for another 20 minutes, or until the Parmesan has started to brown and the peppers are soft. The peppers may have blistered, but that just means the bell pepper is soft enough to melt in your mouth. (If there's any burned skin, it's easy to remove once the bell pepper has cooled enough so you don't burn your hands.)

9. Garnish each pepper with the remaining ¼ teaspoon of Tuscan seasoning. Serve with the pita half. You'll need a knife and fork for this one. And when the saucy mixture oozes out, you'll know this is a winner!

REUSE IT: Store the remaining stuffed bell pepper in an airtight container and refrigerate for up to 3 days. For reimagined leftovers, dump the filling over ¼ cup of grains and slice the bell pepper to mix into the saucy filling. Reheat in the microwave, then top with 1 tablespoon grated Parmesan and some chopped fresh basil.

Per serving: Calories: 381; Total fat: 11g; Carbohydrates: 57g; Fiber: 13g; Protein: 19g; Sodium: 514mg

Ricotta Mac-n-Cheese with Spinach and Marinara

MAKES 2 SERVINGS

ACTIVE TIME: *10 minutes* / **TOTAL TIME:** *15 minutes*

This dish is perfect for when you're craving lasagna. It's simple and quick and has many of the same qualities—zesty, cheesy, and creamy. Note: Béchamel may sound fancy, but this version is foolproof. VEGETARIAN

FOR THE MAC-N-CHEESE

1 cup cooked macaroni elbows

½ cup low-sodium marinara sauce

½ teaspoon garlic powder, divided

¼ teaspoon Tuscan seasoning or Italian seasoning

¼ cup nonfat ricotta cheese

2 tablespoons finely chopped fresh basil or scallion greens

2 cups baby spinach

FOR THE LIGHT BÉCHAMEL SAUCE

¾ cup low-fat milk

1 tablespoon whole-wheat flour

1 tablespoon grated Parmesan cheese

⅛ teaspoon garlic powder

Pinch sea salt

1 tablespoon freshly squeezed lemon juice (optional)

Pinch red pepper flakes (optional)

1. In a medium skillet, combine the cooked macaroni, marinara, ¼ teaspoon of garlic powder, and Tuscan seasoning on medium heat. Give it a good stir and cook for about 5 minutes, until thoroughly warmed.

2. Meanwhile, in a small bowl, mix the ricotta, basil, and remaining ¼ teaspoon of garlic powder. Add the ricotta mixture to the skillet in small dollops, but don't mix.

3. Add the spinach, cover, and heat just until the spinach wilts, about 1 minute. Remove the pan from the heat.

4. To make the béchamel sauce, heat the milk in a small saucepan on medium heat. Whisk in the flour, Parmesan, garlic powder, and salt and whisk constantly until it boils, 1 to 2 minutes. Remove the pan from the heat and stir in the lemon juice (if using).

5. Divide the macaroni mixture between a storage container and a bowl. Pour an equal amount of the béchamel onto each serving. Garnish with red pepper flakes (if using). Seal the storage container and refrigerate for up to 4 days.

REUSE IT: To reheat, transfer the leftovers to a microwave-safe dish, cover partially, and microwave for 1 to 2 minutes. Top with a garnish of finely chopped fresh herbs, if you like.

———————

Per serving: Calories: 291; Total fat: 8g; Carbohydrates: 36g; Fiber: 3g; Protein: 16g; Sodium: 357mg

Scalloped Potatoes with Broccoli and Beans

MAKES 2 SERVINGS

ACTIVE TIME: *10 minutes* / **TOTAL TIME:** *40 minutes*

If you love a rich sauce but don't want to load up on all the fat and calories of a traditional cheesy bake, this one's for you. Scalloped potatoes take a little longer to bake, but the result is delicious. VEGETARIAN

FOR THE POTATOES AND BROCCOLI

Nonstick cooking spray

6 baby potatoes (about 3 ounces), cut into ⅛-inch slices

½ cup vegetable broth

1 cup steamed broccoli florets

1 cup canned low-sodium black beans, warmed

FOR THE CHEESE SAUCE

½ teaspoon extra-virgin olive oil

¼ cup chopped onion

½ teaspoon garlic powder

¼ cup plain low-fat Greek yogurt

¼ cup plus 2 tablespoons low-fat milk

1 tablespoon whole-wheat flour

½ cup shredded low-fat cheddar cheese

1. Preheat the oven to 400°F. Coat a 9-inch baking dish with cooking spray.

2. Put the potatoes in the prepared baking dish and pour the broth over them.

3. Bake for 30 minutes, or until the potatoes are tender when pierced with a fork.

4. Meanwhile, to make the cheese sauce, heat the oil in a small saucepan on medium-low heat for 30 seconds. Add the onion and garlic powder and cook for 3 to 4 minutes, until the onion has softened and is just slightly browned.

5. In a small bowl, whisk together the yogurt, milk, and flour until very few lumps remain. Pour the mixture into the saucepan and add the cheese. Cook, stirring, for 3 to 4 minutes, until the sauce is creamy, thick, and slightly simmering.

6. When the potatoes are done, remove the baking dish from the oven and turn on the broiler.

7. Mix in the steamed broccoli with the potatoes. Pour the cheese sauce over the potatoes and broccoli to evenly coat. Broil for 4 to 5 minutes, until lightly browned.

8. Divide the potato and broccoli mixture between a storage container and a serving dish. Divide the black beans between the two portions, mixed in or on the side. Seal the storage container and store in the refrigerator for up to 4 days.

MAKE IT EASIER: To save yourself 30 minutes of baking time, put the potatoes and vegetable broth in a microwave-safe dish, cover, and microwave for 7 minutes, or until tender. Transfer to the prepared baking dish, add the broccoli, and proceed with step 4.

Per serving: Calories: 351; Total fat: 6g; Carbohydrates: 54g; Fiber: 12g; Protein: 22g; Sodium: 467mg

Shakshuka with Broccoli

MAKES 2 SERVINGS
ACTIVE TIME: *10 minutes* / **TOTAL TIME:** *15 minutes*

With North African and Mediterranean influences, this zesty tomato-based egg dish brings a delightful warmth to your palate. VEGETARIAN

½ cup canned low-sodium crushed tomatoes

¼ cup low-sodium marinara sauce

2 tablespoons water

1 tablespoon salsa

½ teaspoon garlic powder

⅛ teaspoon ground cumin

⅛ teaspoon ground coriander

Pinch sea salt

1 medium egg

1 ounce fresh mozzarella cheese

1 tablespoon chopped scallion greens

Freshly ground black pepper

Red pepper flakes

½ cup steamed broccoli florets

1. In a small nonstick skillet, combine the tomatoes, marinara, water, salsa, garlic powder, cumin, coriander, and salt. Heat on medium-high heat for about 3 minutes, until bubbly and heated through.

2. Crack an egg into the center of the sauce.

3. Crumble bits of the mozzarella and sprinkle the scallions around the contents of the pan.

4. Reduce the heat to medium and cook for about 10 minutes, until the egg white is set, moving the egg white around the simmering sauce with a spoon to ensure it cooks throughout without overcooking the yolk.

5. Season with black pepper and red pepper flakes. Serve half the shakshuka over the broccoli. Store the remaining half in an airtight container in the refrigerator for up to 1 week.

MAKE IT EASIER: Steam the broccoli in a microwave-safe container with 2 tablespoons water, covered, for 3 minutes in the microwave, or reheat leftover broccoli for about 45 seconds to 1 minute in the microwave.

Per serving: Calories: 259; Total fat: 12g; Carbohydrates: 19g; Fiber: 5g; Protein: 17g; Sodium: 455mg

Spaghetti Pomodoro

MAKES 2 SERVINGS

ACTIVE TIME: *5 minutes* / **TOTAL TIME:** *25 minutes*

Save yourself a pot to clean and make this zesty all-in-one pasta dish. Peas add more protein to the dish, so you can eat a little less pasta but get just as much satisfaction. VEGAN

1¼ cups water

1 cup canned low-sodium crushed tomatoes

3 ounces whole-wheat spaghetti

½ cup low-sodium marinara sauce

½ cup frozen peas

2 teaspoons extra-virgin olive oil

1 teaspoon garlic powder

¼ teaspoon dried oregano

⅛ teaspoon sea salt

3 tablespoons chopped fresh basil

1. In a small saucepan, combine the water, tomatoes, pasta, marinara, peas, oil, garlic powder, oregano, and salt.

2. Bring to a boil on medium heat; this will take about 10 minutes.

3. Boil for 12 to 14 minutes, stirring occasionally, until the sauce is thickened and the pasta is al dente.

4. Mix in the basil and serve.

REUSE IT: You'll love the leftovers from this satisfying, flavorful meal. Enjoy half now and store the rest in an airtight container in the refrigerator for up to 4 days.

Per serving: Calories: 334; Total fat: 8g; Carbohydrates: 54g; Fiber: 8g; Protein: 12g; Sodium: 555mg

One-Skillet Farro

MAKES 1 SERVING

ACTIVE TIME: *5 minutes* / **TOTAL TIME:** *25 minutes*

Farro gives this dish a hearty texture and a comforting appeal. Cooking everything together in one skillet allows the grains to absorb all the flavors from the other ingredients. VEGETARIAN

1 teaspoon extra-virgin olive oil	½ cup canned low-sodium crushed tomatoes
½ cup canned low-sodium chickpeas	⅓ cup water
¼ cup chopped zucchini	¼ cup farro
2 tablespoons frozen corn kernels	3 fresh basil leaves, chopped
2 tablespoons chopped scallion greens	2 tablespoons grated Parmesan cheese
½ teaspoon garlic powder	Pinch red pepper flakes (optional)
Pinch sea salt	

1. Heat the oil in a medium nonstick skillet or small saucepan on medium heat for 30 seconds. Add the chickpeas, zucchini, corn, scallions, garlic powder, and salt and cook for about 3 minutes, until the scallions and zucchini are slightly browned.

2. Add the tomatoes, water, farro, and basil. Bring to a boil, then cover, reduce the heat, and simmer for about 15 minutes, until the liquid is absorbed.

3. Garnish with the Parmesan cheese and red pepper flakes (if using).

REUSE IT: Transfer the leftover canned chickpeas and crushed tomatoes to separate airtight containers and store in the refrigerator for up to 4 days. You can add them to soups, salads, and egg scrambles throughout the week.

———

Per serving: Calories: 420; Total fat: 11g; Carbohydrates: 66g; Fiber: 13g; Protein: 18g; Sodium: 456mg

Pasta Primavera

MAKES 1 SERVING

ACTIVE TIME: *10 minutes* / **TOTAL TIME:** *15 minutes*

This vegan dish combines the goodness of fresh zucchini and mixed frozen veggies. Frozen veggies are picked at their peak of ripeness, so they stay nutrient-dense. VEGAN

2 teaspoons extra-virgin olive oil

½ cup frozen mixed veggies (such as peas, carrots, corn, and green beans)

¼ cup chopped onion

¼ cup chopped zucchini

1 teaspoon Tuscan seasoning (or 1 teaspoon Italian seasoning plus pinch red pepper flakes)

⅛ teaspoon sea salt

¼ cup canned low-sodium diced tomatoes, drained, or 1 medium fresh tomato, chopped

½ cup cooked whole-wheat spaghetti

1. Heat the oil in a small saucepan on medium-high heat for 30 seconds.

2. Add the frozen veggies, onions, zucchini, Tuscan seasoning, and salt.

3. Reduce the heat to medium and cook, stirring frequently, for 5 to 7 minutes, until onion is soft and translucent.

4. Add the tomatoes and cook for another minute to heat through.

5. Mix in the pasta and serve.

REUSE IT: Save the remaining diced tomatoes in an airtight container in the refrigerator for up to 4 days. You can use them in your Scrambled Egg in a Mug (page 21).

Per serving: Calories: 322; Total fat: 11g; Carbohydrates: 48g; Fiber: 7g; Protein: 9g; Sodium: 280mg

Egg Roll with a Southwestern Twist

MAKES 1 SERVING

ACTIVE TIME: *15 minutes* / **TOTAL TIME:** *20 minutes*

East meets Southwest: With the veggies, eggs, beans and salsa—all wrapped up in a toasty flour tortilla—it's inspired by an egg roll, but with Tex-Mex appeal.

VEGETARIAN

1 teaspoon extra-virgin olive oil

¼ cup chopped onion or scallion greens

¼ teaspoon garlic powder

Pinch sea salt

1 cup shredded cabbage and carrot blend

¼ cup mixed frozen veggies
(peas, corn, carrots)

1 medium egg

¼ cup canned low-sodium black beans

2 tablespoons salsa

1 (8-inch) **whole-wheat tortilla**

1. Heat the oil in a medium nonstick skillet on medium heat for 30 seconds. Add the onion, garlic powder, and salt and cook, stirring constantly, for 5 to 7 minutes, until the onion is translucent.

2. Stir in the cabbage and frozen veggies and cook for 5 minutes, or until the cabbage is softened.

3. Push the vegetables to one side of the pan and crack the egg on the empty side. Scramble the egg for 1 to 2 minutes, until set. Add the black beans and salsa and stir to combine.

4. Transfer the mixture to a plate. Toast the tortilla in the pan for 1 to 2 minutes, until browned on the bottom. Remove from the pan.

5. Fill the tortilla with the egg, bean, and veggie mixture and fold into a wrap.

REUSE IT: Seal the leftover black beans in an airtight container and refrigerate for up to 4 days.

Per serving: Calories: 387; Total fat: 13g; Carbohydrates: 53g; Fiber: 12g; Protein: 17g; Sodium: 766mg

Veggie and Ground Turkey Skillet

MAKES 1 SERVING

ACTIVE TIME: *20 minutes* / **TOTAL TIME:** *25 minutes*

For this savory veggie turkey dish, you'll make your own simple DIY seasoned gravy in a skillet with the meat and veggies for an efficient 30-minute meal.

1 cup finely chopped cauliflower or frozen cauliflower rice

½ cup frozen mixed veggies (such as corn, peas, carrots, and green beans)

2 teaspoons extra-virgin olive oil

¼ cup chopped onion

2 pinches sea salt, divided

3 ounces lean ground turkey or lean ground beef

½ cup low-sodium chicken broth

1 tablespoon whole-wheat flour

¼ teaspoon Italian seasoning

Freshly ground black pepper (optional)

1. Put the cauliflower and veggies in a microwave-safe dish and pour in about ¼ inch of water. Cover and microwave for 4 minutes. Drain and set aside.

2. Meanwhile, heat the oil in a medium nonstick skillet on medium heat for 30 seconds. Add the onion and a pinch of salt. Cook, stirring frequently, for 3 to 5 minutes, until the onion is translucent.

3. Add the ground turkey and cook, stirring frequently, for about 5 minutes, until fully browned.

4. Stir in the steamed veggies, chicken broth, and flour and cook, stirring constantly, for 3 to 4 minutes, until a gravy has formed.

5. Season with the Italian seasoning, another pinch of salt, and pepper to taste (if using).

MAKE IT EASIER: If you want to skip the cauliflower rice, use a blend of frozen mixed veggies that includes cauliflower and use 1½ cups total.

———

Per serving: Calories: 374; Total fat: 21g; Carbohydrates: 27g; Fiber: 5g; Protein: 20g; Sodium: 427mg

Veggie Burger with Sautéed Bell Peppers and Onions

MAKES 1 SERVING

ACTIVE TIME: *5 minutes* / **TOTAL TIME:** *15 minutes*

A frozen ready-made veggie patty makes this meal semi-homemade. But you'll still get the benefit of cooking your peppers and onions—the appetizing aroma fills the kitchen. VEGETARIAN

1 teaspoon extra-virgin olive oil

1 medium bell pepper (any color), **seeded and sliced**

¼ cup sliced onions

1 veggie patty (look for one with 300 mg sodium or less)

1 small whole-wheat roll, cut in half

1 teaspoon Dijon mustard

1. Heat the oil in a medium skillet on medium heat for 30 seconds.
2. Add the bell pepper and onion and cook, stirring occasionally, for 5 to 7 minutes, until the onion is translucent and the bell pepper is soft. Transfer to a plate.
3. Add the veggie patty to the skillet and heat for 2 to 3 minutes on each side, until fully defrosted and warmed.
4. Meanwhile, lightly toast the wheat roll.
5. To assemble the burger, spread the Dijon on the bottom half of the roll. Add the veggie patty, top with the onion and bell pepper, and then the top of the roll.

HEALTHY HACK: Add lettuce or spinach to your burger to get in some leafy greens.

———

Per serving: Calories: 288; Total fat: 11g; Carbohydrates: 37g; Fiber: 10g; Protein: 18g; Sodium: 664mg

Sweet Potato and Broccoli with Sausage

MAKES 2 SERVINGS

ACTIVE TIME: *5 minutes* / **TOTAL TIME:** *35 minutes*

This dish reminds me of Thanksgiving stuffing, with its variety of texture and hearty flavors. But it also packs in veggies and protein and keeps saturated fats to a minimum.

Nonstick cooking spray

1 cup ½-inch sweet potato cubes

1 cup small broccoli florets

3 precooked turkey sausage breakfast links, sliced, or 1 veggie burger, chopped

½ cup water

½ teaspoon garlic powder

⅛ teaspoon dried rosemary

⅛ teaspoon dried thyme

1 teaspoon extra-virgin olive oil

1. Preheat the oven to 400°F.

2. Coat a 9-inch nonstick baking dish with cooking spray. Add the sweet potato, broccoli, sausages, water, garlic powder, rosemary, and thyme. Drizzle with the oil.

3. Bake for 30 minutes, or until a fork can easily puncture the sweet potatoes.

4. Divide the mixture between a storage container and a bowl. Seal the container and store in the refrigerator for up to 4 days.

REUSE IT: Enjoy the leftovers over a bed of leafy greens with a splash of olive oil and vinegar, or with ½ cup cooked grains.

––––––––

Per serving: Calories: 256; Total fat: 10g; Carbohydrates: 31g; Fiber: 5g; Protein: 11g; Sodium: 307mg

Pan-Seared Salmon
with Balsamic Glaze
p. 78

6. Braise: Add the peas, bell pepper, fennel, vegetable broth, remaining ½ cup of water, remaining 1 teaspoon of garlic, and cinnamon. Cover and cook for 10 minutes, or until most of the liquid is absorbed and the veggies are softened.

7. Serve half the tilapia and veggies over half the cooked quinoa.

REUSE IT: Store the remaining fish, veggies, and quinoa in separate airtight storage containers in the refrigerator for up to 3 days. For a delicious soup, combine the leftover tilapia, veggies, and quinoa in a small saucepan and add ¾ cup vegetable broth and ¾ cup water. Warm over medium-low heat until heated through.

———

Per serving: Calories: 349; Total fat: 9g; Carbohydrates: 31g; Fiber: 9g; Protein: 38g; Sodium: 456mg

Easy Baked Salmon with Lemony Asparagus

MAKES 2 SERVINGS

ACTIVE TIME: *5 minutes* / **TOTAL TIME:** *15 minutes*

This one-pan baked salmon dish is super easy—simply season and bake. Because there's plenty of lemon, you really don't need much salt, if any.

Nonstick cooking spray

1 (8-ounce) **salmon fillet**

20 medium asparagus spears, tough ends trimmed

Pinch sea salt

1 lemon

1 teaspoon extra-virgin olive oil

1. Preheat the oven to 425°F. Line a baking dish with aluminum foil and coat with cooking spray.

2. Put the salmon and asparagus in the prepared pan and season very lightly with salt.

3. Cut the lemon in half. Thinly slice one half. Zest the other half into a small dish and set aside. Generously squeeze the zested lemon half all over the salmon and asparagus. Layer the lemon slices on top, and drizzle with the oil.

4. Bake for 12 to 15 minutes, until the salmon flakes easily with a fork. The residual heat in the pan will keep cooking the salmon after you remove it from the oven. Sprinkle with the lemon zest and serve.

REUSE IT: Store the leftover salmon and asparagus in two separate airtight containers in the refrigerator for up to 2 days. For a refreshing salad, cut up the salmon and asparagus and serve over baby spinach with sliced strawberries.

———

Per serving: Calories: 294; Total fat: 18g; Carbohydrates: 8g; Fiber: 4g; Protein: 27g; Sodium: 143mg

Lemon Pepper Tilapia with Bell Peppers and Potatoes

MAKES 2 SERVINGS

ACTIVE TIME: *5 minutes* / **TOTAL TIME:** *25 minutes*

A combination of scalloped potatoes and delicate steamed tilapia, this one-skillet meal is creamy and satisfying, with a delightful punch from the lemon pepper.

1 tablespoon extra-virgin olive oil

5 baby potatoes, cut into ⅛-inch slices

1 large bell pepper (any color), seeded and sliced

¼ teaspoon garlic powder

1 cup low-fat milk

2 tablespoons whole-wheat flour

1 tablespoon Dijon mustard or 2 tablespoons capers

1 tablespoon freshly squeezed lemon juice

½ teaspoon lemon pepper seasoning, plus more for serving (optional)

⅛ teaspoon sea salt

1 (8-ounce) tilapia fillet

1 cup steamed broccoli florets

1. Heat the oil in a medium skillet on medium heat for 30 seconds. Add the potatoes, bell pepper, and garlic powder and cook, stirring occasionally, for 10 minutes, or until the potatoes are slightly browned and the pepper is tender. Add water as needed to prevent sticking.

2. Add the milk, flour, Dijon, lemon juice, lemon pepper, and salt and cook, stirring constantly, for about 5 minutes, until the liquid begins to thicken.

3. Add the tilapia fillet on top and cover the pan. Cook for 7 to 10 minutes, until the fish flakes apart.

4. Season with additional lemon pepper seasoning, if desired, and serve with the steamed broccoli on the side.

REUSE IT: Store half the fish dish in an airtight container in the refrigerator for up to 3 days. Pan-fry with 1 cup frozen mixed veggies.

Per serving: Calories: 402; Total fat: 12g; Carbohydrates: 35g; Fiber: 3g; Protein: 39g; Sodium: 629mg

Roasted Herb Shrimp
with Chickpeas and Tomatoes

MAKES 1 SERVING

ACTIVE TIME: *5 minutes* / **TOTAL TIME:** *20 minutes*

The seasoning for this dish is quite simple—just olive oil, sea salt, and basil—but the roasting brings out all the flavor! Save time and do less cleanup with this all-in-one-pan meal.

Nonstick cooking spray

2 teaspoons extra-virgin olive oil

1 teaspoon dried basil or 1 tablespoon finely chopped fresh basil

⅛ teaspoon sea salt

4 ounces medium shrimp, peeled and deveined

½ cup canned low-sodium chickpeas

½ cup frozen green beans

2 small tomatoes, diced

⅛ teaspoon freshly ground black pepper

1. Preheat the oven to 425°F. Line a small baking dish with aluminum foil and lightly coat with cooking spray.

2. In a small bowl, whisk together the oil, basil, and salt.

3. Put the shrimp in one half of the prepared baking dish and mix the chickpeas, green beans, and tomatoes in the other half. Pour the herb seasoning over the shrimp.

4. Bake for 12 to 15 minutes, until the shrimp are pink and opaque.

5. Mix the veggies and shrimp, and transfer to a serving dish, scraping any remaining residue from the foil (the seasoning is delicious).

6. Season with the pepper and serve.

REUSE IT: Store the leftover canned chickpeas in an airtight container and refrigerate for up to 4 days. That remaining cup of chickpeas is the exact amount you'll need in the healthy hack option for my Peanut Butter and Chocolate Chip Oatmeal Cookies (page 104).

───────

Per serving: Calories: 348; Total fat: 13g; Carbohydrates: 30g; Fiber: 10g; Protein: 31g; Sodium: 440mg

Lemon-Dijon Salmon

MAKES 2 SERVINGS

ACTIVE TIME: *5 minutes* / **TOTAL TIME:** *20 minutes*

This simple sheet-pan meal cooks in just 15 minutes or less, depending on the thickness of the salmon fillet. The only thing you need to prepare is a simple, tangy lemon-Dijon sauce, and the oven takes care of the rest.

FOR THE LEMON-DIJON SAUCE

2 tablespoons freshly squeezed lemon juice

2 teaspoons extra-virgin olive oil

2 teaspoons Dijon mustard

2 teaspoons maple syrup

FOR THE SALMON AND VEGETABLES

Nonstick cooking spray

1 (8-ounce) **salmon fillet**

1 cup chopped broccoli florets

1 cup chopped cauliflower or cauliflower rice

¼ **cup sliced almonds**

2 tablespoons capers (optional)

1. Preheat the oven to 425°F. Line a small baking dish with aluminum foil and coat lightly with cooking spray.

2. To make the lemon-Dijon sauce, in a small bowl, whisk together the lemon juice, oil, Dijon, and maple syrup until well combined.

3. Put the salmon in one half of the prepared baking dish and mix the broccoli, cauliflower, and almonds in the other half. Pour the Dijon sauce over the salmon.

4. Bake for 12 to 15 minutes, until the salmon easily flakes with a fork. The residual heat in the pan will keep cooking the salmon after you remove it from the oven.

5. Serve half the salmon with half the veggie mixture, garnished with the capers (if using).

REUSE IT: Seal the leftover salmon and veggie mixture in separate airtight containers in the refrigerator. The salmon will keep for up to 3 days, and the cauliflower broccoli mixture will keep for up 4 days. For a reimagined meal, create a salad bowl layered with leafy greens, the chopped salmon, 2 tablespoons chickpeas, and the roasted broccoli-cauliflower combo.

Per serving: Calories: 327; Total fat: 17.5g; Carbohydrates: 13g; Fiber: 4g; Protein: 30g; Sodium: 232mg

Shrimp and Quinoa "Fried Rice"

MAKES 1 SERVING

ACTIVE TIME: *5 minutes* / **TOTAL TIME:** *10 minutes*

If you love fried rice but want to stay heart-healthy, this dish is for you! This version uses only a minimal amount of oil and there isn't any frying. It's also a great way to use up leftover quinoa.

FOR THE SEASONING

1 tablespoon freshly squeezed lemon juice

2 teaspoons extra-virgin olive oil

½ teaspoon garlic powder

¼ teaspoon low-sodium soy sauce

FOR THE SHRIMP AND QUINOA

4 ounces medium shrimp, peeled and deveined

½ cup frozen cauliflower rice or finely chopped cauliflower

½ cup mixed frozen veggies (such as corn, peas, carrots, and green beans)

¼ cup sliced almonds

½ cup cooked quinoa

2 tablespoons chopped scallion greens

1. To make the seasoning, in a small nonstick skillet, whisk together the lemon juice, oil, garlic powder, and soy sauce. Heat on medium-high heat for 30 seconds.

2. Put the shrimp in one half of the skillet and the cauliflower, mixed veggies, and almonds in the other half.

3. Cook the shrimp for 3 minutes on each side, or until pink, opaque, and lightly browned. Stir the veggie mixture in between.

4. Scoop the veggie mixture into a bowl and mix in the quinoa. Top with the shrimp and garnish with the scallions.

REUSE IT: Wrap the leftover cut lemon tightly in plastic wrap and refrigerate for up to 4 days.

———

Per serving: Calories: 405; Total fat: 16g; Carbohydrates: 36g; Fiber: 7g; Protein: 31g; Sodium: 217mg

Seared Ahi Tuna with Ginger-Soy Glaze

MAKES 2 SERVINGS

ACTIVE TIME: *10 minutes* / **TOTAL TIME:** *15 minutes*

Ahi tuna is a bit more costly than tilapia, shrimp, or salmon, so save this recipe for when you want to treat yourself (or perhaps have a guest). Searing tuna requires high heat over a short period of time, so your dish will be ready in minutes.

20 medium asparagus spears, tough ends trimmed

½ cup sliced or chopped sweet potato

¼ cup chopped scallion greens

1 tablespoon extra-virgin olive oil, plus 2 teaspoons

1 tablespoon freshly squeezed lemon juice

1 tablespoon vegetable broth

1 teaspoon maple syrup

½ teaspoon low-sodium soy sauce

¼ teaspoon dried basil

¼ teaspoon garlic powder

⅛ teaspoon ground ginger

1 (8-ounce) ahi tuna steak, cut in half (you can ask the butcher at the fish counter to do this)

Freshly ground black pepper (optional)

1. Put the asparagus in a microwave-safe bowl and pour in about ¼ inch of water. Cover and microwave for 3 to 4 minutes, until tender. Drain the asparagus and divide between two serving plates.

2. Put the sweet potatoes in the same bowl and pour in ¼ inch of water. Cover and microwave for 3 to 4 minutes, until tender. Drain, and divide between the two plates.

3. Meanwhile, to make the ginger-soy glaze, in a small bowl, whisk together the scallions, 1 tablespoon of oil, lemon juice, broth, maple syrup, soy sauce, basil, garlic powder, and ground ginger. Set aside.

4. Heat the remaining 2 teaspoons of oil in a medium skillet over high heat for 1 to 2 minutes, until smoking. Carefully place both tuna pieces in the pan. Sear for 45 seconds on each side and transfer to the serving plates. The tuna should still be pink inside; it will continue to cook a bit after being removed from the heat.

5. Add the glaze to the pan and heat for 1 to 2 minutes, using a spatula to scrape up the flavorful bits from the pan. Pour the glaze over the tuna.

6. Season everything with pepper, if desired, and serve.

REUSE IT: If you don't have a guest for this exquisite meal, seal the remaining tuna in one storage container and the remaining asparagus and sweet potato in another container and store in the refrigerator for up to 3 days. Serve in a chopped leafy green salad with cucumber and tomato, with a squeeze of lemon and a drizzle of olive oil.

Per serving: Calories: 350; Total fat: 13g; Carbohydrates: 26g; Fiber: 6g; Protein: 35g; Sodium: 153mg

Pan-Seared Salmon with Balsamic Glaze

MAKES 2 SERVINGS

ACTIVE TIME: *5 minutes* / **TOTAL TIME:** *15 minutes*

Because searing requires high heat over a short period of time, this fish dish is quick to prepare. Just be sure to turn the fan on, as the balsamic reduction can get steamy.

FOR THE BALSAMIC GLAZE

2 tablespoons balsamic vinegar

1½ tablespoons freshly squeezed lemon juice

2 teaspoons maple syrup

1 teaspoon extra-virgin olive oil

FOR THE SALMON AND GREEN BEANS

2 teaspoons extra-virgin olive oil, divided

1 (8-ounce) **salmon fillet**

2 tablespoons chopped scallion greens, for garnish (optional)

1 cup green beans

2 tablespoons sliced almonds

1 cup cooked quinoa

1. To make the balsamic glaze, in a small bowl, whisk together the vinegar, lemon juice, maple syrup, and oil until well combined.

2. To make the salmon, heat 1 teaspoon of oil in a medium nonstick skillet on high heat for 30 seconds. Add the salmon, skin-side up (if there's skin). Sear each side for 3 to 4 minutes, until browned and cooked through. Transfer to a plate.

3. Add the balsamic glaze to the skillet. It will bubble and steam. Stir constantly for about 1 minute, until it starts to reduce.

4. Pour the balsamic reduction over the seared salmon. Garnish with the scallions (if using).

5. Add the remaining 1 teaspoon of oil to the pan. Reduce the heat to medium and add the green beans and almonds.

6. Cook for 7 minutes, or until the green beans are tender.

7. Serve half the seared glazed salmon with half the green beans and quinoa.

REUSE IT: Seal the leftover salmon in a container and store in the refrigerator for up to 3 days.

———

Per serving: Calories: 410; Total fat: 18g; Carbohydrates: 32g; Fiber: 5g; Protein: 39g; Sodium: 173mg

Sardine Tartine with Chimichurri Pesto

MAKES 2 SERVINGS
ACTIVE TIME: *5 minutes* / **TOTAL TIME:** *5 minutes*

This one's a satisfying no-cook meal for those evenings when you just want something good and hearty, but you also want to take a break from cooking. It's almost as simple as preparing toast, with just one little extra step (making the pesto—literally a minute in your processor).

FOR THE CHIMICHURRI PESTO

1½ cups coarsely chopped fresh basil

¼ cup baby spinach

2 tablespoons walnuts

2 tablespoons extra-virgin olive oil

1 tablespoon freshly squeezed lemon juice

2 teaspoons balsamic vinegar

½ teaspoon garlic powder

⅛ teaspoon sea salt

Pinch red pepper flakes

FOR THE SARDINE TARTINES

1 slice whole-grain bread, toasted

Nonstick cooking spray

1 (3-ounce) can water-packed sardines, drained

Juice of ½ lemon

1 small tomato, sliced

1. To make the chimichurri pesto, in a small food processor, blend the basil, spinach, walnuts, oil, lemon juice, vinegar, garlic powder, and salt until mostly smooth (it can still have some leafy chunks). Stir in the red pepper flakes.

2. Lightly coat the toast with cooking spray. Smash the sardines onto the toast. Squeeze the juice from the lemon half onto the mashed sardines.

3. Generously spread one-third of the pesto over the sardines.

4. Top with the sliced tomato. Cut the tartine in half and store half in an airtight container in the refrigerator; plan to eat it the next day.

REUSE IT: Store the remaining chimichurri pesto in an airtight container in the refrigerator for up to 4 days. A heaping tablespoon of this pesto is great on toast, pasta, or eggs.

Per serving: Calories: 377; Total fat: 21g; Carbohydrates: 22g; Fiber: 4g; Protein: 28g; Sodium: 335mg

Foil-Baked Cod with Lemon-Herb Dressing

MAKES 2 SERVINGS

ACTIVE TIME: *5 minutes* / **TOTAL TIME:** *20 minutes*

For this steamy good eat, a foil wrap produces moist, deliciously seasoned fish. It's also an easy way to cook your protein and veggies all in one.

FOR THE LEMON-HERB DRESSING

1 tablespoon freshly squeezed lemon juice

1 tablespoon extra-virgin olive oil

1 teaspoon garlic powder

⅛ teaspoon Italian seasoning

⅛ teaspoon dried basil or 2 fresh basil leaves, chopped

Pinch sea salt

FOR THE COD, VEGETABLES, AND QUINOA

Nonstick cooking spray

16 medium asparagus spears, tough ends trimmed

1 medium bell pepper (any color), seeded and sliced

1 (8-ounce) cod fillet

2 tablespoons chopped scallion greens

1 cup cooked quinoa

Lemon wedge, for garnish (optional)

Chopped fresh basil, for garnish (optional)

1. Preheat the oven to 425°F.

2. To make the lemon-herb dressing, in a small bowl, whisk together the lemon juice, oil, garlic powder, Italian seasoning, basil, and salt.

3. Cut 2 (12-inch) squares of aluminum foil. Place one piece in a rectangular baking dish. Lightly coat with cooking spray.

4. Layer the asparagus, bell pepper, and cod on top of the foil.

5. Pour most of the lemon-herb dressing over the fish, reserving 1 teaspoon to season the quinoa. Top with the scallions. Place the remaining piece of foil on top and crimp the edges all the way around to seal.

6. Bake for about 15 minutes, until the fish flakes easily with a fork.

7. Season the quinoa with the reserved teaspoon of lemon-herb dressing and divide between a storage container and a serving bowl.

8. Divide the contents of the foil packet between the bowl of quinoa and another storage container. Garnish the bowl with a lemon wedge and basil (if using).

REUSE IT: Store the container of fish and vegetables in the refrigerator for up to 2 days. Store the container of quinoa in the refrigerator for up to 5 days.

————

Per serving: Calories: 311; Total fat: 10g; Carbohydrates: 30g; Fiber: 7g; Protein: 28g; Sodium: 189mg

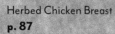

Herbed Chicken Breast
p. 87

CHAPTER SIX

Poultry and Meat

Five-Spice Pork Chops with Chickpea "Fried Rice"

MAKES 2 SERVINGS

ACTIVE TIME: *20 minutes* / **TOTAL TIME:** *30 minutes*

This pork dish features Chinese five-spice powder, a seasoning blend consisting of ground cloves, cinnamon, star anise, Sichuan pepper, and fennel. It infuses the pork with a sweetness that pairs well with the savory blend of soy sauce and garlic.

FOR THE PORK CHOP

2 teaspoons extra-virgin olive oil

½ teaspoon maple syrup or honey

¼ teaspoon garlic powder

⅛ teaspoon Chinese five-spice powder

1 (5-ounce) **boneless pork chop** (1 inch thick)

2 teaspoons low-sodium soy sauce

FOR THE CHICKPEA "FRIED RICE"

2 teaspoons extra-virgin olive oil

1 cup chopped onion

1 medium bell pepper (any color), **seeded and chopped**

¼ teaspoon low-sodium soy sauce

¼ teaspoon garlic powder

¼ teaspoon sea salt

⅛ teaspoon Chinese five-spice powder

1 cup canned low-sodium chickpeas

Freshly ground black pepper

2 tablespoons chopped scallion greens

1. Preheat the oven to 400°F.

2. To make the pork chop, in a small baking dish, mix the oil, maple syrup, garlic powder, and five-spice powder.

3. Add the pork chop and use tongs to fully coat it in the seasoned oil blend.

4. Bake the pork chop for 18 to 20 minutes, until the internal temperature registers 145°F.

5. Transfer the pork chop to a cutting board and cut into ½-inch pieces. Place the baking dish on the stovetop, add the soy sauce, and scrape with a spatula to loosen all the seasoned residue from the bottom. Pour the liquid over the pork chop pieces.

6. While the pork is baking, make the chickpea fried rice. Heat the oil in a medium skillet on medium heat for 30 seconds.

7. Add the onion and sauté for 3 minutes, or until softened. Add the bell pepper, soy sauce, garlic powder, salt, and five-spice powder and cook, stirring occasionally, for 10 minutes, or until the onion and bell pepper are soft.

8. Add the chickpeas, cover, and cook for about 2 minutes, until heated through. Season with pepper.

9. Serve half the pork over half the chickpea "fried rice." Garnish with the scallions.

REUSE IT: Store the leftover pork and chickpea "fried rice" in an airtight container in the refrigerator for up to 3 days.

———

Per serving: Calories: 362; Total fat: 14g; Carbohydrates: 37g; Fiber: 8g; Protein: 25g; Sodium: 555mg

Balsamic and Honey Glazed Pork Chops

MAKES 2 SERVINGS

ACTIVE TIME: *5 minutes* / **TOTAL TIME:** *20 minutes*

So easy and delicious, this seared glazed pork chop goes great with applesauce and seasoned zucchini.

1 (8-ounce) **boneless pork chop**

⅛ **teaspoon dried rosemary**

⅛ **teaspoon sea salt**

2 **teaspoons extra-virgin olive oil**

1 **tablespoon balsamic vinegar**

1 **teaspoon honey**

1 **large zucchini, sliced**

Freshly ground black pepper

½ **cup applesauce, warmed**

1. Season both sides of the pork chop with the rosemary and salt.

2. Heat the oil in a medium skillet on medium-high heat for about 1 minute, until the oil shows small bubbles.

3. Add the pork chop to the hot oil and sear for 5 minutes on each side, or until browned.

4. Transfer the pork chop to a cutting board, let rest for about 5 minutes, and cut into 1-inch pieces.

5. Return the pork to the skillet and reduce the heat to medium. Add the balsamic vinegar and honey and cook, stirring to coat the pork, for about 2 minutes.

6. Transfer the pork and most of the sauce to a plate and cover to keep warm. Add the zucchini to the sauce remaining in the skillet, cover, and cook for 7 minutes, or until tender. Sprinkle with pepper.

7. Serve half the pork and half the zucchini with the applesauce.

REUSE IT: Chop the remaining pork and zucchini into small pieces and store in an airtight container in the refrigerator for up to 5 days. Reheat and mix with ½ cup steamed brown rice and ½ cup heated frozen mixed veggies, topped with 1 tablespoon balsamic vinegar and 1 teaspoon honey.

Per serving: Calories: 288; Total fat: 9g; Carbohydrates: 23g; Fiber: 4g; Protein: 28g; Sodium: 80mg

Herbed Chicken Breast

MAKES 2 SERVINGS

ACTIVE TIME: *5 minutes* / **TOTAL TIME:** *30 minutes*

This chicken dish has a colorful mélange of veggies—red, white, and green. The chicken will finish cooking first, so you'll transfer it to a plate after 20 minutes while continuing to cook the vegetables until the tomatoes blister and the potatoes are softened.

Nonstick cooking spray

1 (6-ounce) skinless, boneless chicken breast

16 medium asparagus spears, tough ends trimmed

1 cup cherry tomatoes

½ cup sliced baby red potatoes

2 teaspoons extra-virgin olive oil

½ teaspoon garlic powder

¼ teaspoon dried thyme

¼ teaspoon sea salt

⅛ teaspoon lemon pepper seasoning or freshly ground black pepper

2 tablespoons chopped scallion greens

1. Preheat the oven to 425°F. Line a small baking dish with aluminum foil and lightly coat with cooking spray.

2. In a resealable plastic bag, combine the chicken, asparagus, tomatoes, and potatoes. Add the oil, garlic powder, thyme, salt, and lemon pepper seasoning. Shake well until everything is thoroughly coated.

3. Dump the contents of the bag into the prepared baking dish and spread out evenly.

4. Bake for 20 minutes, or until the juices run clear when the chicken is sliced and the flesh is no longer pink. Transfer the chicken to a plate and cover with foil to keep warm.

5. Return the baking dish to the oven and bake the veggies for another 10 minutes, or until the tomatoes pucker and the potatoes are soft. The asparagus should be tender and will likely crisp a bit at the tips.

6. Serve half the chicken with half the veggies, garnished with the scallions.

REUSE IT: Serve leftover chicken and veggies over leafy greens for a chopped chicken salad, topped with a splash of vinegar and a drizzle of oil.

———

Per serving: Calories: 331; Total fat: 10g; Carbohydrates: 30g; Fiber: 8g; Protein: 34g; Sodium: 407mg

Teriyaki Pork with Roasted Carrots and Broccoli

MAKES 2 SERVINGS
ACTIVE TIME: *5 minutes* / **TOTAL TIME:** *30 minutes*

Here's a mouthwatering meal that requires very little hands-on time. The pork and vegetables are coated with a simple DIY teriyaki sauce and then baked all together for one-pan ease.

Nonstick cooking spray

1½ cups chopped carrot

1½ cups chopped broccoli florets

1 (6-ounce) boneless pork chop

2 teaspoons extra-virgin olive oil

⅛ teaspoon sea salt

⅛ teaspoon dried basil

1 teaspoon low-sodium soy sauce

1 teaspoon maple syrup

⅛ teaspoon ground ginger

⅛ teaspoon garlic powder

2 tablespoons chopped scallion greens

1. Preheat the oven to 400°F. Line a small baking dish with aluminum foil and lightly coat with cooking spray.

2. In a resealable plastic bag, combine the carrots, broccoli, pork chop, oil, salt, and basil. Shake vigorously and massage until well coated.

3. Dump the contents of the bag into the prepared baking dish and spread out evenly, with the pork chop in the center.

4. In a small bowl, whisk together the soy sauce, maple syrup, ground ginger, and garlic powder to make a glaze. Pour over the pork chop.

5. Bake for 20 minutes, or until the internal temperature of the pork reaches 145°F.

6. If the veggies aren't quite done, transfer the pork to a plate and cover with foil. Continue to bake the veggies for another 5 to 10 minutes, until the texture is to your liking.

7. Cut the pork into ½-inch slices and serve half over the veggie mixture, garnished with the scallions.

———

Per serving: Calories: 261; Total fat: 10g; Carbohydrates: 25g; Fiber: 6g; Protein: 19g; Sodium: 391mg

Italian Wedding Soup

MAKES 1 SERVING

ACTIVE TIME: *5 minutes* / **TOTAL TIME:** *20 minutes*

Warm up to a hearty bowl of nourishment with this version of Italian wedding soup. For practical purposes, I use already cooked meat instead of making from-scratch meatballs.

1 teaspoon extra-virgin olive oil

1 garlic clove, minced

¼ cup chopped onion

½ cup chopped broccoli florets

1 (4-ounce) **cooked turkey burger or 1 leftover cooked Skillet Meatloaf patty** (page 91)

1½ cups low-sodium chicken broth

½ cup water

1 medium egg

1 tablespoon grated Parmesan cheese

⅓ cup cooked farro

Juice of ½ lemon

⅛ teaspoon lemon pepper seasoning

⅛ teaspoon Tuscan seasoning (or ⅛ teaspoon Italian seasoning plus pinch red pepper flakes) (optional)

1. Heat the oil and garlic in a small saucepan on medium heat for 30 seconds.

2. Add the onion and cook for 7 minutes, or until it starts to soften. (If needed, add a splash of chicken broth to prevent sticking.)

3. Stir in the broccoli and cook for another 2 minutes. Crumble the cooked turkey burger into the pan.

4. Add the chicken broth and water and bring to a boil, which will take about 10 minutes.

5. In a small bowl, whisk together the egg and Parmesan until smooth.

6. Once the water reaches a gentle boil, gently drizzle in the egg mixture and stir with a fork for about 1 minute, until white egg ribbons form.

7. Add the cooked farro, lemon juice, lemon pepper, and Tuscan seasoning (if using).

REUSE IT: This is a great vehicle for using leftover grains and/or cooked ground meat—just be sure to swap for equal portions as noted in the recipe.

Per serving: Calories: 441; Total fat: 25g; Carbohydrates: 28g; Fiber: 4g; Protein: 31g; Sodium: 535mg

Turkey Chili

MAKES 1 SERVING

ACTIVE TIME: *5 minutes* / **TOTAL TIME:** *25 minutes*

With chickpeas, corn, mushrooms, and tomato, this chili packs in plenty of heart-healthy ingredients. And it's very satisfying, too!

1 teaspoon extra-virgin olive oil

¼ cup chopped onion or 1½ teaspoons onion powder

¼ cup chopped mushrooms

4 ounces ground turkey or 1 turkey burger patty

½ cup low-sodium chicken broth

⅓ cup low-sodium marinara

¼ cup canned low-sodium chickpeas

¼ cup frozen corn

2 tablespoons tomato paste

1 teaspoon Tuscan seasoning (or 1 teaspoon Italian seasoning plus pinch red pepper flakes)

½ teaspoon garlic powder

½ teaspoon low-sodium Worcestershire sauce or low-sodium soy sauce

⅛ teaspoon ground cumin

1 to 2 tablespoons chopped scallion greens (optional)

1. Heat the oil in a medium saucepan on medium heat for 30 seconds. Add the onion and cook for 7 minutes, or until it starts to soften. (If needed, add a splash of chicken broth to prevent sticking.)

2. Stir in the mushrooms and cook for 2 minutes, or until tender.

3. Add the turkey and cook, breaking up the meat with a spoon or spatula, for 5 minutes, or until no longer pink.

4. Mix in the chicken broth, marinara, chickpeas, corn, tomato paste, Tuscan seasoning, garlic powder, Worcestershire sauce, and cumin and cook for 5 minutes, or until heated through.

5. Garnish with the scallions (if using).

HEALTHY HACK: Add a handful of raw spinach when the chili is almost done. Cover for 2 minutes, or until the spinach has wilted.

———

Per serving: Calories: 404; Total fat: 21g; Carbohydrates: 36g; Fiber: 8g; Protein: 22g; Sodium: 434mg

Skillet Meatloaf

MAKES 2 SERVINGS

ACTIVE TIME: *5 minutes* / **TOTAL TIME:** *20 minutes*

Get your meatloaf fix with this simple stove-top recipe—it requires only a skillet with a lid and less than 30 minutes of your time. I like to serve it with ½ cup cooked barley (or other leftover grains) and steamed green beans.

½ cup low-sodium ketchup

2 teaspoons low-sodium Worcestershire sauce

1 teaspoon onion powder

½ teaspoon garlic powder

8 ounces ground turkey

2 tablespoons bread crumbs or rolled oats

2 tablespoons Parmesan cheese

⅛ teaspoon sea salt

2 teaspoons extra-virgin olive oil

¼ cup chicken broth

1 tablespoon chopped fresh parsley (optional)

1. In a small bowl, mix the ketchup, Worcestershire sauce, onion powder, and garlic powder until well combined.

2. Transfer 2 tablespoons of the seasoned ketchup to a medium bowl and add the turkey, bread crumbs, Parmesan, and salt. Mix well with your hands and form into two plump patties, each about 1½ inches thick.

3. Heat the oil in a nonstick skillet on medium heat for 30 seconds.

4. Add the seasoned turkey patties and heat for 1 minute on each side, or until browned.

5. Pour in the broth, cover, and reduce the heat to medium-low. Cook for about 15 minutes, until fully cooked. Transfer the patties to a plate.

6. Pour the remaining seasoned ketchup into the pan and heat on low for 2 minutes, or until warmed.

7. Pour the warmed seasoned ketchup over the meatloaf patties.

REUSE IT: Store one patty in an airtight container in the refrigerator for up to 4 days. You can use it in my Spaghetti Bolognese (page 92) or Italian Wedding Soup (page 89).

―――――

Per serving: Calories: 339; Total fat: 16g; Carbohydrates: 25g; Fiber: 1g; Protein: 25g; Sodium: 427mg

Spaghetti Bolognese

MAKES 2 SERVINGS

ACTIVE TIME: *5 minutes* / **TOTAL TIME:** *20 minutes*

If you've got any leftover Skillet Meatloaf (page 91), it will be perfect for this recipe. Otherwise, fresh lean ground beef is just fine. The mushrooms add their own "meatiness," so you'll be eating less red meat.

2 teaspoons extra-virgin olive oil

1 cup chopped mushrooms

¼ cup chopped onion

6 ounces lean ground beef

1 cup low-sodium marinara sauce

2 tablespoons low-sodium chicken broth, divided

¼ teaspoon low-sodium Worcestershire sauce

Pinch sea salt

½ cup cooked pasta

½ cup steamed broccoli

¼ teaspoon dried parsley, for garnish

1. Heat the oil in a medium nonstick skillet on medium heat for 30 seconds.

2. Add the mushrooms and onion and cook for 5 minutes, or until the onion has started to soften. (If needed, add a splash of chicken broth to prevent sticking.)

3. Add the ground beef and cook, breaking up the meat with a spoon or spatula, until no longer pink, about 5 minutes.

4. Add the marinara, broth, Worcestershire sauce, and salt and cook, stirring occasionally, for 5 minutes, or until the sauce is thickened.

5. Serve half the meat sauce over the pasta, with the steamed broccoli on the side.

6. Garnish with the parsley.

REUSE IT: Store the remaining meat sauce in an airtight container in the refrigerator for up to 4 days.

Per serving: Calories: 444; Total fat: 22g; Carbohydrates: 34g; Fiber: 7g; Protein: 30g; Sodium: 290mg

Savory Stuffed Sweet Potato with Sausage and Broccoli

MAKES 1 SERVING

ACTIVE TIME: *5 minutes* / **TOTAL TIME:** *30 minutes*

Sausage is a perfect pairing for sweet potato, giving it a sweet-savory appeal. An herbed ricotta blend pulls it all together, and a couple of tablespoons of pistachios add a nice flavor and crunch to the meal—and an additional 3 grams of protein.

Nonstick cooking spray

1 large sweet potato, well scrubbed

½ cup chopped broccoli florets

2 precooked turkey sausage breakfast links

2 tablespoons nonfat ricotta cheese

1 tablespoon low-sodium chicken broth

2 teaspoons extra-virgin olive oil, divided

½ teaspoon Italian seasoning

2 tablespoons pistachios

1. Preheat the oven to 400°F. Line a rimmed baking sheet with aluminum foil and lightly coat with cooking spray.

2. Poke the sweet potato all over with a fork and put it in a microwave-safe bowl. Pour in about ¼ inch of water, cover, and microwave for 7 to 10 minutes, until fully cooked.

3. When cool enough to handle, cut the sweet potato in half and scoop out about 2 tablespoons from each side. Place the halves on the prepared baking sheet, side by side.

4. Fill the hollows of the sweet potato with the broccoli and sausage.

5. In a small bowl, mix the ricotta cheese, broth, 1 teaspoon of oil, and Italian seasoning until creamy and smooth.

6. Divide the ricotta blend between both halves of the stuffed potato.

7. Drizzle the remaining 1 teaspoon of oil on top. Sprinkle on the pistachios.

8. Bake for 20 minutes, or until the cheese is slightly browned.

REUSE IT: Serve extra sweet potato with 2 teaspoons ricotta cheese or hummus and season with dried rosemary or Italian seasoning.

———

Per serving: Calories: 440; Total fat: 23g; Carbohydrates: 41g; Fiber: 8g; Protein: 20g; Sodium: 341mg

Turkey Burger with DIY Special Sauce

MAKES 1 SERVING

ACTIVE TIME: *5 minutes* / **TOTAL TIME:** *15 minutes*

It's the special sauce that makes this burger so zesty and delicious! A simply seasoned patty with crisp lettuce, tomato, and a slathering of sauce is all you need for one satisfying meal.

1 (4-ounce) **turkey burger patty**

Freshly ground black pepper

Nonstick cooking spray

2 tablespoons hummus

1 teaspoon **sweet pickle relish**

1 teaspoon Dijon mustard

1 teaspoon low-sodium ketchup

1 small whole-wheat hamburger bun

1 romaine lettuce leaf

1 small tomato, sliced

1. Season the turkey burger patty generously with pepper.

2. Lightly coat a small nonstick skillet with cooking spray.

3. Put the patty in the skillet and cook on medium heat for 6 minutes on each side, or until no longer pink.

4. While the patty is cooking, in a small bowl, mix together the hummus, relish, Dijon, and ketchup until well combined. Spread onto both sides of the hamburger bun.

5. Sandwich the patty, lettuce, and tomato in the sauce-coated bun.

HEALTHY HACK: Have two medium mandarin oranges for dessert to get in half your day's dose of vitamin C, which aids in iron absorption.

———

Per serving: Calories: 356; Total fat: 14g; Carbohydrates: 31g; Fiber: 6g; Protein: 28g; Sodium: 822mg

Skillet Chicken Pot Pie

MAKES 2 SERVINGS

ACTIVE TIME: *15 minutes* / **TOTAL TIME:** *25 minutes*

Crustless it may be, but it's got all the taste, comfort, and satisfaction you'd expect from a chicken pot pie!

2 teaspoons extra-virgin olive oil

1 medium carrot, chopped

1 small celery stalk, chopped

¼ cup chopped onion

1 (6-ounce) skinless, boneless chicken breast

¼ teaspoon sea salt, divided

1 tablespoon whole-wheat flour

1 cup low-sodium chicken broth

½ cup mixed frozen veggies (such as carrots, peas, corn, and green beans)

½ teaspoon Italian seasoning

¼ teaspoon low-sodium Worcestershire sauce

Freshly ground black pepper or lemon pepper seasoning (optional)

½ cup steamed brown rice

1. Heat the oil in a medium nonstick skillet on medium for 30 seconds.

2. Add the carrot, celery, and onion and cook, stirring occasionally, for 3 minutes. (If needed, add a splash of broth to prevent sticking.)

3. Season both sides of the chicken with ⅛ teaspoon of salt.

4. Add the seasoned chicken to the skillet and cook for 2 minutes on each side.

5. Add the flour and stir around into the veggies. Add the broth, frozen veggies, Italian seasoning, Worcestershire sauce, and remaining ⅛ teaspoon of salt and bring to a boil.

6. Cover and cook for 5 minutes, or until the chicken is tender and no longer pink. Remove the chicken from the pan and continue to let the sauce thicken.

7. Cut the chicken into chunks and stir them into the gravy and veggie mixture. If desired, season with pepper to taste.

8. Serve half the chicken and vegetable mixture over the rice.

HEALTHY HACK: Serve with ½ cup steamed broccoli florets for additional calcium and fiber.

———

Per serving: Calories: 348; Total fat: 9g; Carbohydrates: 41g; Fiber: 4g; Protein: 26g; Sodium: 404mg

Crispy Coated Chicken with Zucchini and Carrots

MAKES 2 SERVINGS
ACTIVE TIME: *5 minutes* / **TOTAL TIME:** *35 to 40 minutes*

This crispy chicken is coated with two kinds of nuts—almonds and pistachios—for both crunch and flavor! Fun fact: Pistachios contain 6 grams of protein per ounce.

1½ tablespoons extra-virgin olive oil

1 medium egg

2 tablespoons buttermilk

2 tablespoons whole-wheat flour

2 tablespoons crushed pistachios

2 tablespoons crushed almonds

⅛ teaspoon sea salt

1 (6-ounce) skinless, boneless chicken breast, cut in half

Nonstick cooking spray

½ cup chopped carrot

½ cup chopped zucchini

1. Preheat the oven to 425°F. Line a baking dish with aluminum foil and spread the oil in the bottom.

2. In a shallow bowl, whisk together the egg and buttermilk until smooth.

3. In another shallow bowl (or a large resealable plastic bag), combine the flour, pistachios, almonds, and salt.

4. Dunk the chicken pieces fully in the egg mixture to coat.

5. Transfer the chicken to the flour mixture and toss completely until well coated. (If using a bag, seal and shake vigorously.)

6. Put the coated chicken in the prepared baking dish. Pour the remaining flour-nut mixture on top. Spray with cooking spray.

7. Scatter the carrots and zucchini around the chicken.

8. Bake for 20 minutes, or until the chicken is no longer pink. Transfer the chicken to a plate.

9. Continue to bake the veggies for another 10 to 15 minutes, until soft.

10. Store half the chicken and vegetables in an airtight container in the refrigerator for up to 5 days.

MAKE IT EASIER: Use frozen carrot medallions instead of fresh so you can skip step 9. Because frozen veggies are already blanched before being frozen, they soften much more quickly in the oven.

Per serving: Calories: 369; Total fat: 23g; Carbohydrates: 14g; Fiber: 3g; Protein: 27g; Sodium: 164mg

One-Pot Chicken and Pasta Soup

MAKES 2 SERVINGS
ACTIVE TIME: *5 minutes* / **TOTAL TIME:** *25 minutes*

This soup is so easy, you just toss all the ingredients in a pot and heat it up. Did you know that couscous is actually a tiny pasta, not a grain?

2 cups low-sodium chicken broth

1 (6-ounce) skinless, boneless chicken breast

½ medium bell pepper (any color), seeded and chopped

½ cup chopped zucchini

⅓ cup couscous

¼ cup chopped onion

2 teaspoons extra-virgin olive oil

1 teaspoon Italian seasoning

¼ teaspoon sea salt

¼ teaspoon garlic powder or 1 garlic clove, minced

1. In a small saucepan, combine the broth, chicken, bell pepper, zucchini, couscous, onion, oil, Italian seasoning, salt, and garlic powder.

2. Cook on medium heat for about 20 minutes, until the chicken is no longer pink. Transfer the chicken to a cutting board and cut into pieces, then return them to the pan.

3. Serve half now and store the remaining portion in an airtight container in the refrigerator for up to 4 days.

REUSE IT: Wrap the remaining bell pepper half in plastic wrap and store in the refrigerator for up to 2 days. For a simple healthy snack, fill it with 2 to 3 tablespoons nonfat ricotta and add a few grinds of black pepper.

———

Per serving: Calories: 315; Total fat: 9g; Carbohydrates: 31g; Fiber: 3g; Protein: 29g; Sodium: 411mg

Turkey Burger Sloppy Joe with EZ Coleslaw

MAKES 2 SERVINGS

ACTIVE TIME: *10 minutes* / **TOTAL TIME:** *20 minutes*

This savory meat sauce is so good, you'll want to sop up every last bit. If you don't want to use a bun, you can serve the sloppy joe mixture over ½ cup leftover grains.

FOR THE SAVORY MEAT SAUCE

2 teaspoons extra-virgin olive oil

½ cup chopped onion

1 (5-ounce) turkey burger patty

1 cup low-sodium marinara sauce

½ teaspoon low-sodium Worcestershire sauce

½ teaspoon garlic powder

1 whole-wheat hamburger bun

FOR THE EZ COLESLAW

¼ cup low-fat plain Greek yogurt

Juice of 1 lemon

1 tablespoon extra-virgin olive oil

1 teaspoon apple cider vinegar

1 teaspoon honey

⅛ teaspoon sea salt

1½ cups shredded cabbage or cabbage-carrot blend

1. To make the savory meat sauce, heat the oil in a medium nonstick skillet on medium heat for 30 seconds. Add the onion and sauté for 5 minutes, or until softened.

2. Push the onion to the edges of the pan and place the turkey burger patty in the center. Cook the patty for 6 minutes on each side, or until no longer pink.

3. When the patty is done, break it up into small chunks with a spatula and mix into the onion. Add the marinara, Worcestershire sauce, and garlic powder and heat through.

4. While the turkey is cooking, make the EZ coleslaw. In a medium bowl, whisk together the yogurt, lemon juice, oil, vinegar, honey, and salt. Add the cabbage and stir until well combined.

5. Serve half the sloppy joe mixture in the bun, with half the coleslaw on the side.

REUSE IT: For a reimagined meal, serve the meat sauce over pasta (such as macaroni or couscous) with the coleslaw mixed into a bed of spinach greens.

––––––––

Per serving: Calories: 380; Total fat: 21g; Carbohydrates: 29g; Fiber: 5g; Protein: 19g; Sodium: 460mg

Sausage and Onions with Warm Curried Cabbage

MAKES 1 SERVING

ACTIVE TIME: *10 minutes* / **TOTAL TIME:** *25 minutes*

To create the well-rounded flavor of the curried slaw, this dish combines the sweetness of apples and cranberries with the tang of Dijon, Worcestershire, and vinegar. It's a perfect accompaniment to the hearty flavors of the sausage and onions.

2 teaspoons extra-virgin olive oil, divided

⅛ teaspoon sea salt

2 cups shredded cabbage or cabbage-carrot blend

½ medium apple, cored and chopped

1 tablespoon dried cranberries

½ teaspoon balsamic vinegar

¼ teaspoon Dijon mustard

¼ teaspoon curry powder

2 tablespoons water

Freshly ground black pepper

1 teaspoon extra-virgin olive oil

¼ cup chopped onion

2 precooked turkey sausage breakfast links

1. Heat 1 teaspoon of oil and the salt in a medium nonstick skillet on medium heat for 30 seconds. Add the cabbage, apple, cranberries, vinegar, Dijon, and curry powder and cook, stirring, for 5 minutes.

2. Add the water, cover, reduce the heat to low, and cook for 5 minutes, or until the cabbage and apples are soft. Transfer the mixture to a plate and season with pepper to taste.

3. In the same skillet, heat the remaining 1 teaspoon of oil on medium heat for 30 seconds. Add the onion and sauté for 5 minutes, or until softened.

4. Add the sausages and cook for about 3 minutes on each side, until browned. Serve the sausages and onions with the warm slaw on the side.

MAKE IT EASIER: Replace the cabbage with spring greens or baby spinach and add all the other slaw ingredients (except the water). Toss together as a traditional (room-temperature) salad. Add a squeeze of lemon if you like.

Per serving: Calories: 419; Total fat: 23g; Carbohydrates: 41g; Fiber: 7g; Protein: 17g; Sodium: 697mg

Skillet Peach Crisp
p. 113

CHAPTER SEVEN

Divine Desserts

Peanut Butter and Chocolate Chip Oatmeal Cookies

MAKES 8 COOKIES

ACTIVE TIME: *5 minutes* / **TOTAL TIME:** *15 minutes*

Make a small batch of chewy chocolate chip cookies, enjoy two, and freeze the rest for later. These delicious chocolate chip cookies are egg-free and gluten-free (if you use GF-certified oats), with less refined sugar than your traditional cookie. VEGETARIAN

Nonstick cooking spray

½ cup canned low-sodium chickpeas

2 tablespoons maple syrup or 6 small pitted dates

¼ cup unsweetened coconut flakes

1 tablespoon peanut butter

1½ teaspoons vegetable oil

¼ teaspoon vanilla extract

Pinch sea salt

¼ cup rolled oats

1 to 3 teaspoons water

3 tablespoons chocolate chips

2 tablespoons crushed walnuts

1. Preheat the oven to 375°F. Lightly coat a rimmed baking sheet with cooking spray or use a nonstick baking sheet.

2. In a high-speed blender or food processor, blend the chickpeas and maple syrup until mostly smooth (slightly chunky is okay). Transfer to a small mixing bowl. (Alternatively, you can mash the chickpeas by hand. This will require a fork and a bit of elbow grease. Add the maple syrup a little at a time to keep the mixture moist as you mash.)

3. Stir in the coconut flakes, peanut butter, oil, vanilla, and salt until creamy. Mix in the oats. If the dough is too crumbly and doesn't hold together, add a bit of water, 1 teaspoon at a time, to ensure it comes together. Gently fold in the chocolate chips and walnuts, and do your best to distribute them evenly throughout.

4. Scoop 8 dollops of the cookie dough onto the baking sheet. Lightly coat each with cooking spray to promote browning. Bake for 8 to 10 minutes, until set and slightly browned.

5. Enjoy two and store the remaining cookies in an airtight container in the freezer for up to 1 month.

MAKE IT EASIER: Swap out the chickpeas for ¼ cup flour and use maple syrup. That way you won't need a blender/processor (or any elbow grease).

Per serving (2 cookies): Calories: 216; Total fat: 12g; Carbohydrates: 25g; Fiber: 4g; Protein: 4g; Sodium: 78mg

Brownie in a Mug

MAKES 1 SERVING

ACTIVE TIME: *5 minutes* / **TOTAL TIME:** *5 minutes*

This dessert is truly decadent, yet it takes just minutes to make. You'll get your brownie fix without the hassle of prepping and cleanup (or a tray load of chocolate temptation). VEGETARIAN

Nonstick cooking spray	1 tablespoon vegetable oil
2 tablespoons whole-wheat flour	1 tablespoon low-fat milk
1 tablespoon unsweetened cocoa powder	1 teaspoon chocolate chips
1 tablespoon granulated sugar	2 walnut halves, crushed (optional)

1. Lightly coat the inside of a coffee mug with cooking spray. Add the flour, cocoa, sugar, oil, and milk and mix until well combined.

2. Fold in the chocolate chips. Fold in the walnuts (if using).

3. Microwave for 1 minute 15 seconds, or until the batter is moist and cakelike. If it's still doughy, pop it back in for just a few seconds more—up to a maximum of 15 more seconds.

HEALTHY HACK: Use just 1 teaspoon sugar and mix a few slices of very ripe banana into the batter. (This version will likely require a full 1 minute 30 seconds in the microwave.)

————

Per serving: Calories: 274; Total fat: 16g; Carbohydrates: 32g; Fiber: 3g; Protein: 4g; Sodium: 15mg

Ricotta Cheesecake Parfait

MAKES 1 SERVING

ACTIVE TIME: *5 minutes* / **TOTAL TIME:** *5 minutes*

Get the glorious taste of cheesecake with more protein and less added sugar in this made-for-one parfait! It's a softer, deconstructed version of cheesecake, with the crust crumbled on either the bottom or the top (you decide). VEGETARIAN

3 heaping tablespoons nonfat ricotta cheese

3 heaping tablespoons low-fat plain Greek yogurt

1 tablespoon low-fat cream cheese

1 teaspoon honey

1 teaspoon melted coconut oil (optional)

¼ teaspoon vanilla extract

⅓ cup fresh or frozen berries

1 graham cracker square (½ rectangular sheet)**, crumbled**

1. In a small bowl, combine the ricotta, yogurt, cream cheese, honey, coconut oil (if using), and vanilla. Use a spoon to mix the ingredients well, mashing the cream cheese into the sides of the bowl for a better blend.

2. Layer into a small cup with berries and graham cracker crumbles.

MAKE IT EASIER: If you use whipped cream cheese, you'll find it's much easier to blend.

Per serving: Calories: 256; Total fat: 13g; Carbohydrates: 23g; Fiber: 1.5g; Protein: 13g; Sodium: 155mg

Sweet Cannoli Blintz

MAKES 2 SERVINGS

ACTIVE TIME: *5 minutes* / **TOTAL TIME:** *5 minutes*

This multicultural treat was inspired by the Italian cannoli with its creamy ricotta cheese, but I made it easier by using a Southwestern wrap—the tortilla! Pistachios and dates give it a Middle Eastern feel. And funny enough, it tastes like a Eastern European blintz. VEGETARIAN

¼ cup nonfat ricotta cheese	2 small pitted dates, finely chopped
2 tablespoons low-fat plain Greek yogurt	1 teaspoon extra-virgin olive oil
2 tablespoons low-fat cream cheese	1 (8-inch) whole-wheat tortilla
1 teaspoon honey	1 tablespoon pistachios or almonds
¼ teaspoon ground cinnamon, divided	

1. In a small bowl, combine the ricotta cheese, yogurt, cream cheese, 1 teaspoon of honey, and ⅛ teaspoon of cinnamon. Use a spoon to mix the ingredients well, mashing the cream cheese into the sides of the bowl for a better blend. Fold in the dates. Set aside.

2. Heat the oil in a small nonstick skillet on medium heat for 30 seconds.

3. Place the tortilla in the skillet (it's okay if it needs to fold up a little on the sides), add the ricotta filling in the center, and let the tortilla brown for 1 minute.

4. Using a spatula, remove the tortilla from the skillet and carefully roll it up into a wrap. Place it seam-side down in the pan and heat for another minute or so, until lightly browned.

5. Transfer the blintz to a plate and sprinkle the pistachios on top. Dust with the remaining ⅛ teaspoon of cinnamon. Slice in half.

REUSE IT: Store the remaining half in an airtight container in the refrigerator for up to 2 days. With 9 grams of protein and 3 grams of fiber, it's perfect for breakfast the next day!

Per serving: Calories: 202; Total fat: 9g; Carbohydrates: 25g; Fiber: 3g; Protein: 9g; Sodium: 175mg

Blueberry-Mango Soft-Serve

MAKES 1 SERVING

ACTIVE TIME: *5 minutes* / **TOTAL TIME:** *5 minutes*

Just fruit times three, that's it! Blueberries, mango, and banana make a great combo for this simple frozen treat. It's perfect for a hot, sunny day! **VEGAN**

1 small frozen banana, sliced

½ cup frozen wild blueberries

¼ cup frozen mango chunks

Combine the banana, blueberries, and mango in a blender and process. Turn off as needed and stir with a silicone spatula to get the banana chunks well incorporated for a smooth treat. Serve immediately.

MAKE IT EASIER: The smaller you slice the banana, the easier it will be to process without the frozen banana getting caught in the blades. Taking time in between processing to stir will ensure the best consistency. Note: Do not add water—it will make the mixture too runny.

———

Per serving: Calories: 148; Total fat: 1g; Carbohydrates: 37g; Fiber: 5g; Protein: 1.5g; Sodium: 3mg

Frozen Banana

MAKES 1 SERVING

ACTIVE TIME: *5 minutes* / **TOTAL TIME:** *5 minutes*

This frozen banana treat works whether you slice the banana and drizzle on the chocolate or insert a Popsicle stick handle to roll it in the gooey decadence. For the latter, it's easiest to insert the stick in the banana half before freezing. VEGETARIAN

1½ tablespoons pistachios

3 tablespoons chocolate chips

½ frozen banana

1. Put the pistachios in a small resealable plastic bag. Press out the air and seal. Use a canned food item to crush the nuts into small pieces. Spread out on a small plate.

2. Put the chocolate in a small microwave-safe bowl and microwave for 1 to 2 minutes, stirring every 30 seconds, until melted and smooth.

3. If you've got a Popsicle stick in your banana, roll it around in the melted chocolate and then roll it in the crushed pistachios. Otherwise, slice the banana into ½-inch pieces and drizzle the chocolate on top, then sprinkle on as many pistachios as you can.

REUSE IT: Because chocolate can get sticky, melt more than you actually need to ensure you will have about a tablespoon leftover. Same for the pistachios—crush slightly more than you need. Pour the remaining crushed nuts on top of the melted chocolate. Cover tightly with plastic wrap to seal well, then freeze for up to 3 weeks. You'll have a nice little portion of chocolate bark to enjoy as a treat on another day.

Per serving: Calories: 252; Total fat: 13g; Carbohydrates: 34g; Fiber: 3g; Protein: 3g; Sodium: 1mg

Cinnamon Pita Chips with Honey-Sweetened Ricotta

MAKES 1 SERVING

ACTIVE TIME: *5 minutes* / **TOTAL TIME:** *15 minutes*

Make your own pita chips and enjoy them for dessert, served with creamy ricotta for dipping. (And you score 4 grams of fiber and 13 grams of protein with this simple, tasty treat!) VEGETARIAN

1 medium whole-wheat pita, cut into 8 triangles

1 teaspoon extra-virgin olive oil

⅛ teaspoon sea salt

¼ teaspoon ground cinnamon

Nonstick cooking spray

¼ cup nonfat ricotta cheese

1 teaspoon honey

1. Preheat the oven to 350°F. Line a rimmed baking sheet with aluminum foil.

2. In a resealable plastic bag, combine the pita triangles, oil, and salt. Shake vigorously to coat well.

3. Place the pita triangles in a single layer on the prepared baking sheet. Sprinkle with the cinnamon and lightly coat with cooking spray.

4. Bake for 8 to 10 minutes, flipping halfway through, until crisp.

5. Put the ricotta in a small bowl for dipping, and add a drizzle of honey to sweeten.

MAKE IT EASIER: Spread the ricotta, oil, honey, cinnamon, and salt on top of a whole pita. Place it on the prepared baking sheet and bake for 10 minutes. You'll have a treat you can enjoy however you please—roll it up like a wrap or cut it into wedges.

————

Per serving: Calories: 300; Total fat: 10g; Carbohydrates: 41g; Fiber: 4g; Protein: 13g; Sodium: 446mg

Skinny Bananas Foster

MAKES 1 SERVING

ACTIVE TIME: *5 minutes* / **TOTAL TIME:** *5 minutes*

This dessert is a made-for-one delight. Bananas are sautéed to a light golden crisp and deglazed with the sweet tang of mandarin juice. This delightful combo is served up over a combo of yogurt and ricotta cream. VEGETARIAN

¼ cup low-fat plain Greek yogurt

¼ cup nonfat ricotta cheese

1 teaspoon honey

⅛ teaspoon vanilla extract

1 teaspoon extra-virgin olive oil

1 small banana, sliced

Juice of 1 medium mandarin orange or 2 tablespoons orange juice

1. In a small bowl, whisk together the yogurt, ricotta, honey, and vanilla until creamy.

2. Heat the oil in a nonstick skillet on medium heat for 30 seconds.

3. Add the banana slices in a single layer in the skillet and cook for 1 to 2 minutes, until the bottoms are lightly browned.

4. Squeeze in the mandarin juice to deglaze the pan and use a spatula to scrape up any of the delicious sticky residue, for about 30 seconds.

5. Immediately pour the bananas and syrup over the yogurt-ricotta cream.

MAKE IT EASIER: Use just ½ cup ricotta or ½ cup yogurt. Honestly, I think the combo tastes best, but it will save you a trip to the store if you have only one or the other.

———

Per serving: Calories: 320; Total fat: 11g; Carbohydrates: 45g; Fiber: 4g; Protein: 14g; Sodium: 83mg

Skillet Peach Crisp

MAKES 1 SERVING

ACTIVE TIME: *5 minutes* / **TOTAL TIME:** *5 minutes*

Skillet-warmed peaches served over a light, crunchy granola crisp and topped with a dollop of ricotta make for one satisfying treat! VEGETARIAN

2 tablespoons rolled oats

1 teaspoon whole-wheat flour

1 tablespoon maple syrup

2 teaspoons vegetable oil, divided

1 teaspoon ground cinnamon (optional)

½ cup drained canned peach slices (packed in 100 percent juice)

2 tablespoons nonfat ricotta cheese

1. In a small bowl, mix the oats, flour, maple syrup, and 1 teaspoon of oil. Transfer to a small nonstick skillet and heat on medium-low heat for about 2 minutes, stirring occasionally to break up the pieces, until toasty. Dust with the cinnamon (if using). Return the mixture to the same bowl.

2. Heat the remaining 1 teaspoon of oil in the same skillet on medium heat for 30 seconds.

3. Add the peaches and cook for about 2 minutes, until warmed.

4. Pour the peaches into the bowl with the crisp oat mixture.

5. Top with the ricotta.

REUSE IT: Seal the remaining canned peaches in their juice in an airtight container and store in the refrigerator for up to 5 days.

———

Per serving: Calories: 277; Total fat: 12g; Carbohydrates: 38g; Fiber: 3g; Protein: 6g; Sodium: 39mg

Skillet Crepe with Stewed Blueberries

MAKES 1 SERVING

ACTIVE TIME: *5 minutes* / **TOTAL TIME:** *10 minutes*

Who knew crepes were so easy to make? Sweetened with a warm blueberry compote, they're absolutely divine. VEGETARIAN

FOR THE STEWED BLUEBERRIES

½ cup frozen wild blueberries

Juice of 1 small mandarin

1 teaspoon honey

⅛ teaspoon vanilla extract

FOR THE CREPE

2 tablespoons whole-wheat flour

1 medium egg

2 tablespoons low-fat milk

3 tablespoons water

2 teaspoons vegetable oil, divided

⅛ teaspoon sea salt

2 tablespoons nonfat ricotta cheese (optional)

1. To make the stewed blueberries, in a small saucepan, combine the blueberries, mandarin juice, honey, and vanilla. Heat on medium heat for 2 to 3 minutes, until small bubbles form around the outer edges of the berries. Turn off the heat and cover the pan.

2. To make the crepe, in a small mixing bowl, whisk together the flour and egg. Slowly add the milk and continue to stir until smooth. Mix in the water, 1 teaspoon of oil, and salt.

3. Heat the remaining 1 teaspoon of oil in a small nonstick skillet on medium-high heat for 30 seconds. Pour in the batter and swirl the skillet to evenly coat the entire bottom. Heat for 2 minutes, or until browned on one side. Flip and heat the other side for about 20 seconds.

4. Transfer the crepe to a plate, top with the stewed blueberries, and add the ricotta (if using) to garnish. Roll it up and enjoy with a knife and fork.

MAKE IT EASIER: Prepare the crepe and immediately transfer it to a plate, then use the same skillet to make the stewed blueberries.

―――――――――

Per serving: Calories: 283; Total fat: 15g; Carbohydrates: 30g; Fiber: 2g; Protein: 9g; Sodium: 365mg

Measurement Conversions

	US STANDARD	US STANDARD *(ounces)*	METRIC *(approximate)*
VOLUME EQUIVALENTS *(Liquid)*	2 tablespoons	1 fl. oz.	30 mL
	¼ cup	2 fl. oz.	60 mL
	½ cup	4 fl. oz.	120 mL
	1 cup	8 fl. oz.	240 mL
	1½ cups	12 fl. oz.	355 mL
	2 cups or 1 pint	16 fl. oz.	475 mL
	4 cups or 1 quart	32 fl. oz.	1 L
	1 gallon	128 fl. oz.	4 L
VOLUME EQUIVALENTS *(Dry)*	⅛ teaspoon		0.5 mL
	¼ teaspoon		1 mL
	½ teaspoon		2 mL
	¾ teaspoon		4 mL
	1 teaspoon		5 mL
	1 tablespoon		15 mL
	¼ cup		59 mL
	⅓ cup		79 mL
	½ cup		118 mL
	⅔ cup		156 mL
	¾ cup		177 mL
	1 cup		235 mL
	2 cups or 1 pint		475 mL
	3 cups		700 mL
	4 cups or 1 quart		1 L
	½ gallon		2 L
	1 gallon		4 L
WEIGHT EQUIVALENTS	½ ounce		15 g
	1 ounce		30 g
	2 ounces		60 g
	4 ounces		115 g
	8 ounces		225 g
	12 ounces		340 g
	16 ounces or 1 pound		455 g

	FAHRENHEIT (F)	CELSIUS (C) *(approximate)*
OVEN TEMPERATURES	250°F	120°C
	300°F	150°C
	325°F	180°C
	375°F	190°C
	400°F	200°C
	425°F	220°C
	450°F	230°C

Index

Acknowledgments

I'd like to thank my patients, who've entrusted me with their single-living health challenges, allowing me to keep my advice both practical and suitable for their solo needs. Thanks to my mom for her eagerness to test my recipes; to my husband, JP, and daughters, Ailish and Julia, who have been great sports with several weeks' worth of "tapas" for dinner; to my sister, Rhonda, for always being my cheerleader; and lastly, to my editor and namesake, Lauren, who kept me inspired to do my best work.

About the Author

LAUREN O'CONNOR, MS, RDN, is a registered dietitian/nutritionist, yoga instructor, and three-time cookbook author. She offers nutritional counseling and consulting services for individuals and companies nationwide. A member of the Academy of Nutrition and Dietetics (AND) and Food & Culinary Professionals (FCP), she received her master's degree in nutritional sciences from California State University, Los Angeles.

O'Connor promotes whole-food choices to best suit her clients' needs. With a specialty in gastroesophageal reflux disease (GERD) management, she promotes dietary and lifestyle practices to improve health outcomes for those with acid-reflux concerns. Learn more about her services at NutriSavvyHealth.com.